D1002211

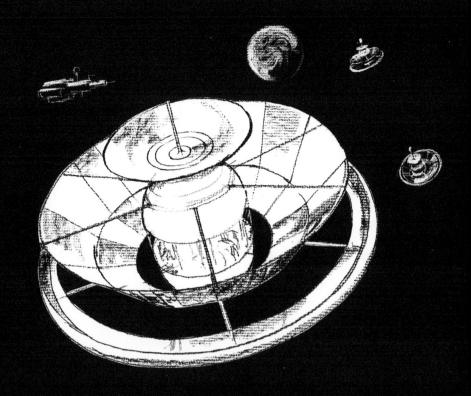

Colonies in Space

Frederic Golden

Colonies

Illustrated with photographs and with drawings by Kiyo Komoda

n Space

The Next Giant Step

 Harcourt Brace Jovanovich, New York and London

Printed in the United States of America

First edition

B C D E F G H I J K

Library of Congress Cataloging in Publication Data

Golden, Frederic.
     Colonies in space.

     Bibliography: p.
     Includes index.
     SUMMARY: Discusses a space-colonization program
being developed by physicist Gerard K. O'Neill which
includes complete living and industrial facilities
operating on solar energy.
     1. Space colonies—Juvenile literature.   2. O'Neill,
Gerard K.—Juvenile literature.   [1. Space colonies.
2. O'Neill, Gerard K.]   I. Komoda, Kiyoaki.
II. Title.
TL795.7.G64   629.44′2   76-46784
ISBN 0-15-219400-2

To all the dreamers and prophets, past
and present, who have pointed the way

It may be that the old astrologers had the truth exactly reversed when they believed that the stars controlled the destinies of men. The time may come when men control the destinies of the stars.

—Arthur C. Clarke, testifying
before Congress, July 1975

Contents

Colonies in Space

Introducing
Project Sunflower

When the little note came in the morning's mail that day in May 1974, my first thought was to toss it into the wastebasket. It was an invitation from Princeton University to attend a day-long meeting on, of all things, space colonization. "Pipe dreams," I muttered to myself. Didn't those people at Princeton know that as a science writer I was concerned with present-day realities— like the last Skylab mission that had been concluded only a few weeks earlier? Fortunately, though, I resisted my initial impulse, to add to that day's pile of garbage, and out of some passing curiosity, I began to look into what was happening at Princeton.

Let me confess first, openly and unashamedly, that I am something of a professional skeptic. It's the natural inclination of most journalists—especially those prowling the precincts of science. And I think the public profits from it; for otherwise our newspapers, magazines, and television and radio programs would be filled with even more absurdities—instant solutions to the energy "crisis" that violate basic physical laws, miraculous overnight cures for cancers, mysterious ship-swallowing triangles in the sea, shenanigans about extraterrestrials landing in UFOs in some Kansas cornfield. So my immediate inclination was to dismiss the idea as daffy when I heard that a Princeton physicist and some of his young colleagues were seriously thinking about establishing extraterrestrial colonies—not on the surface of the moon or Mars, as countless science-fiction writers have done in their reveries, but in the interplanetary void itself at a kind of gravitational hollow called L5.

Yet as I examined their proposals in detail and looked at the scientific credentials of their leader, my skepticism slowly weakened—much to my own surprise. For one thing, Professor Gerard K. O'Neill was not simply another physicist, but one of considerable distinction, who had already made a mark for himself by designing a new type of atom smasher that I had myself written about (alas, without mentioning his name). More important, I mustered every possible objection that I could think of: Do we have the technological skills for such a huge undertaking? What about the dangers of meteoroid hits or cosmic rays? Could people really survive in the maddening, lonely isolation of deep space? Yet O'Neill replied with such thoroughness, plausibility, and conviction as to make it clear that the scheme was much more than a flight of fancy. Indeed, I became so impressed that I wrote several articles about O'Neill for *Time*, then decided his ideas were worthy of lengthier discussion.

Quite obviously, this book is not a comprehensive treatment. Nor is it burdened with technical details that would not interest the ordinary lay reader. I also leave many questions unanswered. For instance, I really can do no more than guess how the colonies—O'Neill prefers the word "habitats" since it smacks less of exploitation—will be governed or how the mineral spoils of the lunar surface or the asteroids will be divided up; possibly we will have a world government by then.

My approach has been chronological. After the opening chapter's letter from the future, I go back in time to tell how O'Neill's proposal evolved and how he had been preceded by other farsighted writers and scientists. In the course of these reflections, I have also touched briefly on some of the high points of the United States space program, notably the extraordinary flight of Skylab—whose full significance as a landmark for living in space has yet to be fully appreciated by a now blasé public. I next explain, step by step, how the first colonies might be built and what life on them might be like. Though I have indulged occasionally in possibly fanciful speculation—predicting, for instance, the development of 3-D television, which might or might not amuse the colonists—almost everything that is described here is well within the reach of our technological ability. Don't look for antigravity machines, instantaneous transporters, or any of the other stock-in-trade devices of science-fiction writers.

Despite my fascination with the concept, I don't mean to suggest that establishing the first colony will be easy. Nor do I think it is likely to happen in the next decade or two, although I would be pleased if it did. Indeed, even the most fervid supporters of colonization, and their number is growing (witness the proliferation of L5 societies in many cities), acknowledge that there are enormous hurdles still to be overcome. Not the least of these is the government's quite proper resistance to any new massive space effort that smacks even remotely of another aerospace boondoggle.

Lately, however, the idea of space colonization has acquired a new argument in its favor that should impress even reluctant Congressmen and hardheaded bureaucrats. It appears that the colonies not only offer endless room for human expansion but also could quickly pay for themselves by helping Earth meet its energy needs. Using the raw material of the moon, the colonists could fabricate giant solar collectors at L5. These celestial power stations could then be towed back toward Earth and placed in fixed orbits, like weather satellites, from which they would beam down microwaves. These, in turn, could be easily converted into electricity. Impossible? Apparently even the no-nonsense engineers of the National Aeronautics and Space Administration do not think so; they are already studying ways of going about this project.

Solar power, in fact, could become so central to the success of space colonization that it suggests a name for the L5 program. It could be called Project Sunflower, after the giant plant that grows so vigorously in bright sunlight that it seems to be reaching out toward our warming star. The name would also symbolize the warm, humanistic—indeed, almost anti-big-technology—attitude of the project's advocates. As it happens, one of the preliminary designs that has been suggested for the first colony actually looks like a member of the genus *Helianthus;* around the central living area are arrays of mirrors that resemble a sunflower's petals.

Whether it is called Project Sunflower or something else, space colonization may not germinate in my lifetime or in that of the youngest reader of this book. But the time frame isn't really all that important. What counts is that the space-colony concept—which could be crucial to humanity's future—receive thoughtful, serious consideration.

No book is the product of the author alone, and this one is certainly no exception. It profited from the advice and interest of many people, but I would like to express special thanks to my editors at *Time,* notably Leon Jaroff, who tolerated—bemusedly, I suspect—my exploration of a subject that must have seemed at first hopelessly far-fetched; Peter Waller of NASA's Ames Research Center, who provided invaluable guidance in this and other projects involving space; Les Gaver, NASA's audio-visual chief, who graciously made available many of the pictures in this book; Florence Helitzer, formerly of Princeton University's information office, who first drew my attention to the subject of space colonization; Dr. Jerry Grey of the American Institute of Aeronautics and Astronautics, who provided wise counsel; members of the L5 Society, who invited me to their meetings and encouraged me with their enthusiasm; Dr. Charles Holbrow of Colgate University, co-editor of the invaluable NASA/Ames/ Stanford 1975 Summer Study; and, most important of all, Dr. Gerard K. O'Neill, without whose inspiration, friendship, and guidance this book would not have been possible.

F.G.

1

A Space Colonist's Journal

10 July 2030, Beta Colony

After weeks of impatient waiting, the great day came almost as an anticlimax.

The lift-off from Cape Canaveral in the Advanced Space Shuttle was quite different from anything I had expected. No deafening roar, no frightening vibrations or large g forces. Unlike the thundering old Saturn 5 rockets we've all seen on videotapes from the first days of the space age, the shuttle was no more uncomfortable than a high-speed elevator.

Climbing rapidly skyward, we reached our low-orbit altitude of 185 kilometers (115 miles) above Earth in scarcely ten minutes. Like many of the other passengers aboard, I felt slightly queasy from the first sensation of weightlessness. But zero-g wasn't a problem for long. Soon the shuttle rendezvoused with the Orbital Transfer Station, a huge wheel-like structure that glistened in the sunlight. It vaguely reminded me of the space station in that amusing old film *2001: A Space Odyssey*—though, of course, it was hardly so primitive.

We entered the station through a docking port in the wheel's hub and were quickly ushered into elevators that swept us through the wheel's spokes and out to the rim. Inside the tunnel-like structure are located the station's living quarters, kitchens, biomedical facilities, and workshops. The floor is so positioned that if you could look out overhead, you would be facing the wheel's hub.

The reason for this seemingly odd geometry is quite simple. As the wheel slowly rotates in space, its motion sets up centrifugal forces somewhat like those one feels when a car or train swerves around a corner. By precisely controlling this rate of rotation, that station's managers can create for those living and working inside the rim a sensation of weight exactly equal to the pull exercised by Earth's gravity.

Ushered into a large, gleaming reception hall decorated with murals of stars, galaxies, and other space scenes, we were formally welcomed by a briefing officer and told what to expect at the station. Our stay there would be about six days. We had already spent three agonizing weeks in isolation on Earth prior to departure so that doctors could determine whether we were incubating any germs that might contaminate the colony. Though the quarantine was exasperating, it makes good medical sense. Like all people who live apart from the rest of the world for long periods, the colonists tend to lose their natural immunity to foreign germs. They would be particularly vulnerable to some new Earth bug.

The briefing officer told us that we would undergo one final checkup before embarking. We also would get additional instructions on the dos and don'ts of living in space. As if that weren't enough, we're also slated for some final psychological tests and one more precautionary debugging for any stray insects, molds, fungi, or germs that might have stowed away on our bodies or clothing. Clearly, even as mankind makes a new world for itself, it isn't about to give up old habits: we're still saddled with all the forms and red tape so dear to the hearts of bureaucrats.

There was one aspect of our stay in the orbital station that was sheer delight. We were expected to exercise regularly in the station's hub. There, because it is located right at the axis of rotation, we experienced virtually no weight. And so this area of the station makes an ideal zero-g gym, where we can practice coping with the weightlessness that we'll encounter when we are working outside the space colony or traveling to another nearby colony.

The orbital station is so thronged with people that it resembles a busy metropolitan hotel. It's also quite a melting pot; though English seems to be the main language, it is spoken with every conceivable accent. Some of the people in our orbital hotel are on their way back to space after home leaves. Others, like myself, are making their first journey to the colonies. The station bustles for another reason: it is a major transfer point for heavy equipment, machinery, and raw materials that are being shipped between Earth, the moon, and the colonies.

Though the first colonies were built nearly forty years ago, they still depend on Earth for certain essential materials that cannot be mined on the moon. These include carbon for high-precision metallurgy, nitrogen for making fertilizers, and, perhaps most important of all, hydrogen. Shipped in cold, liquid form, the hydrogen is combined with oxygen obtained from the moon's rocks to make water. Just thinking of that effort makes one cautious about wasting even a drop of water, though, of course, everything is recycled, and even spilled water will eventually be retrieved.

Right on schedule, we left the station aboard the giant space tug *Jules Verne*. It is named after the nineteenth-century French sci-fi writer who quaintly imagined a trip to the moon in a giant cannon shell. The tug is one of five such large cylinder-shaped ships that regularly ply the triangular route between Earth, the moon, and the colonies at L5. Located in the moon's orbit, L5 is a kind of gravitational pocket that moves roughly at a distance of 386,000 kilometers (240,000 miles) behind the moon as it travels around Earth. Anything that happens to be placed at L5 remains permanently trapped there unless it is towed away by rocket power. Since L5 travels with the moon in its orbit, it also remains at a relatively constant distance of 386,000 kilometers from Earth—the same distance as Earth to moon.

As we headed toward our rendezvous with L5, we made ourselves comfortable aboard the *Jules Verne*. Capable of carrying several hundred passengers, it vaguely reminds me of those great luxury liners that once crossed the Atlantic Ocean. Everyone sleeps in cabins with two or four berths, which are located on both sides of long passageways through the cylinder. At each end of the ship, there are several lounges and a dining hall, where meals are served at several sittings. Somewhat frustratingly, I found very few windows to provide a view of space. But this omission is understandable. The designers were eager to furnish the passengers with as much shielding as possible against bombardment by cosmic rays. Before the era of space exploration, people often worried that a ship might be struck by a large meteoroid. But this is one of the really minor hazards of space travel; the chances of a paralyzing hit by such a large object are far less than those of being struck by lightning while standing outdoors on Earth during an electrical storm or being attacked by a shark while swimming in the ocean. A far greater peril is tiny, invisible cosmic rays, which consist mostly of high-energy protons and electrons and can do damage to human cells.

But we were not shut out from the universe entirely. All the lounges had holovision units, a cross between television and holography—that familiar form of three-dimensional photography. These provided surprisingly vivid, realistic views of space whenever the captain wanted to show us anything interesting that was being picked up with the external cameras. He was a rather charming English-speaking Russian; once, when we were far enough away from Earth, he proudly pointed out the great land mass of Siberia. Unfortunately, for most of the trip, the only things showing on the holovision were old 3-D movies.

Propelled by the high-speed expulsion of fine bits of lunar debris rather than by the exhaust of old-style chemical rockets, the big ship moved so quietly and smoothly through space that we were unaware of any motion whatsoever. Even the cylinder's controlled rotation, which creates a comfortable artificial gravity for everyone on board, was tolerable. Perhaps it's just as well that we didn't have many external windows: it would be a dizzying sensation to be looking out on a world where the stars are constantly spinning.

The *Jules Verne* reached L5's vicinity after about five days, roughly the time it took the old transatlantic liners to make the trip from New York to Southampton. We knew we were approaching the end of our journey from the tug's position on the Space Locator, a kind of miniature planetarium in the main lounge that gave us the position of the ship in relation to the moon, Earth, and L5 throughout the trip.

During the rendezvous and docking, the captain switched off the old movies and showed what was happening outside on the holovision. At first we saw only a glint of light against the dark background of stars. Then the glint turned gradually into a thin, bright band. It was sunlight reflecting off one of the giant solar generators that are being assembled at L5 for future use as power stations above Earth.

Finally Beta Colony itself came into view. It is shaped like a wheel; in fact, it is quite similar to the Orbital Transfer Station, except it is far larger. The original design traces back to a summer study held at Stanford University many years ago; hence it is known to engineers as a Stanford torus.

The entire torus, or wheel, is slightly more than a mile in diameter. Radiating out from the central hub are six spokes,

A completed wheel-shaped colony that houses some 10,000 people. The lunar debris on the wheel's exterior serves as shielding against cosmic rays. The smaller of the two central spheres is the colony's original construction "shack"; the large rectangular-shaped object protruding from it is a radiator that sheds excess heat from the colony. The smaller free-floating ring is a collection mirror that reflects sunlight onto the rings of mirrors within the wheel. These, in turn, reflect the rays into the colony's living and agricultural areas. Some distance from the colony is its manufacturing center for processing lunar ore. (*National Aeronautics and Space Administration*)

each about 15 meters (16 yards) in diameter. A large, tilted mirror sits above the spokes; it is so angled that it reflects sunlight directly onto banks of smaller mirrors around the hub. These in turn reflect light into the outer ring, where the colony's people live and where they grow their crops.

The wheel is not the only shape used in space-habitat design. Some colonies have the form of cylinders. Others are simply spheres. In fact, the variety of designs adds interest to life in space. Traveling between colonies that are so markedly different on the inside and outside is like going from a flat desert region to the mountains or seaside on Earth.

The *Jules Verne* edged slowly but accurately into the docking module, which is part of the wheel's hub. As we approached, we momentarily caught a glimpse of the large mirror on the holovision monitor and had an all-too-fleeting view of the colony's interior. One could see immediately that it was lush with greenery. The ship moved so cautiously that we hardly felt a quiver when the docking locks snapped into place. Our Russian captain had an expert hand. Moments after that operation, the tug's doorways swung open, and we entered Beta Colony.

The welcoming formalities were refreshingly brief; apparently efficiency is absolutely essential in the manpower-shy colonies. While we waited for our luggage, one of the colony's officers checked off our names on his lists and assigned us to our quarters. There were no speeches or tedious instructions; he merely gave each of us a little pamphlet with maps, names, and a brief description of the colony's facilities. Then he wished us well and sent us on our way.

In the colony's hub, as in the center of the orbital station, we felt no sensation of weight. To keep us from floating about, the colony's designers had equipped the hub area with handholds, and it was padded to prevent bruising accidents. I was glad we had had some preliminary exercises in coping with zero-g. But the colony's oldtimers did not seem bothered at all by the effects. In fact, some of them were thoroughly enjoying themselves in the hub's zero-g by playing a kind of local version of touch football. The competitors did not slam into one another but drifted around like swimmers in an underwater ballet.

To get to the colony's living and working areas, we strapped

A large space tug approaching two space colony cylinders with a cargo of supplies and passengers. (*From* Science Year, The World Book Science Annual, *Copyright 1975, Field Enterprises Educational Corporation*)

ourselves into high-speed elevators and rode out in the spokes. Each is nearly half a mile long, about twice the height of the tallest skyscrapers on Earth, so it was quite a ride. As we progressed, we could feel our weight increasing, so, in a sense, we were actually riding "down." Finally, when we reached the rim, we were back at normal weight. It wasn't the effect of real gravity, of course; our weight was due to the wheel's rotation in

A closeup view of a docking port for incoming and departing spacecraft in the central area of a wheel-shaped space colony. Each of the spokes contains elevators that carry people to the habitat areas of the wheel's rim. The large directional antenna is for communicating with Earth or other distant bases. (*National Aeronautics and Space Administration*)

space. However the trick was achieved, it felt good to move normally again.

Despite all the briefings, we had not been fully prepared for the impact of our first encounter with the colony's main working and living areas. Contrary to expectations, we found a bustling, thriving community lined with flowers and trees, almost a gardenlike setting. Along the wheel's curved walls, small bungalow-type apartments are neatly stacked. Though nearly 10,000 people are now living in the wheel, everything has been so well proportioned that there is no sense of overcrowding.

There are many open spaces. Sunshine pours in from large overhead windows, bathing everything in a bright yellow light. Though there are some shops along the tree-lined walkways, most stores, as well as utilities and workshops, are hidden out of sight underneath the street level. Unlike Earth cities, the colony has no skyscrapers or traffic jams. It also has no soot or smog. Everywhere one looks, there are small parks. To get about, most people walk or ride bicycles. But for longer trips, there are remote-controlled electric cars that ride on a track some distance up the sloped wall, somewhat like a monorail. It is an unexpectedly pleasant—one might even say beautiful—little world.

My own quarters in one of the terraced apartment blocks consist of a large living room with foldaway bed, a small kitchen, toilet and shower, and a patio for sunbathing and growing plants. It is, I'm told, a typical bachelor apartment. Married people have larger quarters, usually with at least one extra bedroom for every child. (There is no restriction on the number of children, but since both parents are usually working, the colony's families tend to be limited to no more than two or three youngsters.) The furniture is pleasantly contemporary; the colors are pale pastels. Because wood and plastics are not readily available at the colony—it takes scarce hydrocarbons to make plastics—most of the furnishings are made out of ceramic materials. All in all, it is really quite lovely.

Before settling in, I decided to take a stroll. Everywhere I looked, the colony seemed to be awash with the rich colors of flowers and other foliage. Walking along the main pathway, I encountered clusters of youngsters playing familiar games; basketball is a favorite because the playing facilities take less room than those of football or baseball. I imagine a golfer might be a little disappointed, but I understand that another colony has set up a driving range.

From the people I see everywhere, it seems clear that the colony has a young population. Space is still largely the calling of vigorous, pioneering types. But I notice that there is also a smattering of middle-aged people. Already, many youngsters have been born in space; there have also been some deaths. But all this is to be expected if we are to re-create in space the normal rhythms of everyday life on Earth.

As I continued my walk through the enclosed circular world that is my new home, the colony's interior structure became more clear. The designers have divided it into six separate compartments; there are three residential areas interspersed by three agricultural areas. In part, these divisions are a safety feature, like the bulkheaded compartments of a boat; if a disaster struck in any of these sections—a fire, say, or an outbreak of infection, or even a highly unlikely meteoroid hit—the colony's controllers could quickly isolate the area and start the process of control and repair. If the problem were serious enough, they might ask for the help of nearby colonies. But the main reason for these divisions is to let the colonists create especially favorable growing conditions in the agricultural areas, which are carpeted with moon soil. These areas have atmospheres that are somewhat richer in carbon dioxide and water vapor; they also are subjected to much more sunlight. By such climate manipulation, the colony's growers get three or four crops a year.

Passing through an airlock into one of these areas, I saw how ingeniously the colony's designers have made use of their space to get maximum growing room. Different types of plants are grown on different levels. Such major crops as corn, rice, soybeans, and alfalfa are raised on the main or bottommost level. Higher up along the curved walls is a second level that includes enclosures for chickens, rabbits, and a few cows; the latter are kept not so much for beef as for milk. The topmost level has just enough area for such crops as grapes, berries, and other fruits; it also holds some small fish ponds, where the colonists have even managed to raise such aquatic delicacies as shrimp and lobsters.

A farmer and his young helper at L5 tend to their livestock and crops. Hogs and chickens are easier to raise than beef cattle.

Unlike farms on Earth, there is little of the mess or stench that we usually associate with agriculture. Most of the so-called dirty work—the processing of the animals, for example—is done below street level. Besides, by keeping such activities in separate sections, virtually sterile conditions can be maintained.

Before turning back to my apartment, I stopped briefly at a little shop for a snack (my first taste of colony food was strawberry ice cream). There I found several colonists taking a short break from their work. One of them, a plumbing specialist, told me he had lived at Beta for more than a year and was thinking of signing up for another two-year hitch when his current stay comes to an end. In fact, he said, he didn't miss Earth at all. He had not only made many new friends but had also taken part in many recreational activities. Among other things, he pointed out, the colony has a large variety of clubs for different hobbies—photography, theater, painting, and so forth. It also has a well-stocked library, two radio stations (one for classical, one for popular music), a newspaper that is delivered daily as a printout from the colony's television system, and two gymnasiums: one that operates at normal gravity and another with zero-g, where even the most difficult exercises can become ridiculously easy.

The colony's principal activities, of course, are not amusement. One of its important functions is the construction of orbital power stations for Earth. This is the activity that I am engaged in; my specialty is electrical engineering. Most of the fabrication occurs some distance away from the colony at a site that can only be reached by little shuttle cars precisely aimed at the manufacturing area. Even before I arrived, a large station was already taking shape. Looking like a huge shield, it will use great sheets of silicon cells (somewhat like those in the light meters of cameras) on its exterior surface to convert sunlight directly into electricity; an adjoining power center then converts the electricity into microwaves. When the plant is completed, it will be towed to Earth, placed in a geosynchronous orbit (one in

A resident at L5 enjoys the view of the colony from his comfortable and spacious personal quarters.

which the satellite appears to hover over the same spot on the surface below), and beam down the energy that it captures from sunlight.

Such power stations are an ideal energy source. Nonpolluting, tapping sunlight directly, and operating almost entirely by remote control, they can continue to provide electricity for Earth's power grids for years. Only occasional maintenance visits are required. Because the accumulation of solar energy for Earth is such an important function of the colony, some people have taken to calling the entire program Project Sunflower. It's an apt nickname, for few plants thrive so well in bright sunlight as this tall yellow bloom. In addition, the flower produces seeds and oil that are both edible.

Besides building power stations for Earth, the colony has another essential goal: the construction of another colony—in effect, a carbon copy of the original. The work is already under way, but it will take years to complete. It is easy to see why all the colonies are busily at work replicating themselves. If every colony at L5 gives birth to a new one, the number of colonies will rapidly increase, doubling every few years. In fact, after only a generation or so, there could well be thousands of additional colonies. The only real limit is how fast building materials can be delivered from the moon.

Before the end of the twenty-first century, there could well be millions of people living at L5; some might even begin to think about relocating in more distant places, perhaps millions of miles from Earth. And why not? Even in my brief stay here, I can see that it's a good life in space.

This imaginary journal of a space colonist in the twenty-first century may seem to be just another piece of science fiction; in fact, it is more than that. Many scientists are convinced not only that our next great space step should be aimed at establishing colonies, but that we already have the basic technological knowhow to begin the preliminary work.

The recent feats of science and its immediate offshoot technology support their bold optimism. Consider, for example, the age-old dream of powered flight. After many futile attempts it was finally realized in 1903, when Orville and Wilbur Wright managed to get aloft for a few seconds in a rickety wire-and-stick airplane at Kitty Hawk, North Carolina. Yet only sixty-six years after that first faltering ascent, two astronauts reached the moon—enabling Neil Armstrong to take his memorable "one small step for a man, one giant leap for mankind."

That was only a beginning, however. Unmanned spacecraft, crammed with computers and other complex electronic gear, have now explored all the planets out to Jupiter. In 1976, as part of the American bicentennial celebration, two Viking spacecraft emblazoned with the Stars and Stripes landed on Mars. Among other goals, the billion-dollar expedition sought to settle a question that has nagged astronomers for centuries: Is there life—any life, perhaps even microbes—on the red planet? Still another robot ship is speeding to a rendezvous in the early 1980s with the ringed planet Saturn, while other equally ambitious voyages are in various stages of planning. These include probes into the dense, hot atmosphere of Venus, a close-up look at one of those occasional visitors to our part of the solar system from the far reaches of space—a comet—and journeys to the most distant known member of the sun's family of planets, Pluto.

How will unmanned rocket ships, with only limited fuel supplies, make such far-flung voyages through the interplanetary void? One trick already used by space engineers is to tap the gravitational energy of the planets themselves. Thus, after a spacecraft leaves the Earth, it will use the outer planets as stepping stones, letting the gravity of one hurl it on toward the next until it finally sweeps past Pluto.

Most of these enterprises involve robots, some of them so ingeniously designed that they can virtually think for themselves. And, of course, they will have to; sending a command from Earth to a spaceship in the vicinity of Mars can take nearly twenty minutes—much too long for instructions to arrive in time if there is an emergency that requires an immediate decision. When a spacecraft is among the outer planets, it will take hours for radio signals to reach it, to say nothing of the time required to send a reply back to Earth.

Yet, extraordinary as the computerized spacecraft capable of such journeys may be, they are nonetheless machines. Eventually, in spite of the current reluctance to spend money on space extravaganzas, humans will want to make similar voyages. Not only the moon but more distant planets will become targets of human exploration.

One important initial step toward that goal is already being taken by the United States. This is the creation of a new space vehicle called the space shuttle. A cross of rocket, glider, and conventional aircraft, the shuttle will be able to carry passengers—including civilians who have had no extensive astronaut training—into orbit around the Earth at only a fraction of the cost of the Apollo program's Saturn rockets. Exactly how the National Aeronautics and Space Administration (NASA) expects to achieve this cost-cutting miracle is explained later, but there is nothing complicated about the shuttle's potential payoff. If it works as expected, it will greatly reduce the expense of manned missions to the moon, Mars, or more remote places in the solar system.

Perhaps equally important, the space shuttle will give us the technological capability to take another awesome step in the conquest of space: the establishment of the first colonies or habitats away from Earth.

No one, of course, can say for sure whether progress in space, or, for that matter, in any other area of scientific or technological endeavor, will continue at the present rate. But if the past is any guide to the future, we can surely expect to see more spectacular wonders. The space colonies of Project Sunflower may well be among them.

This cutaway view of an early space shuttle shows scientists at work inside a space lab that will be carried aloft by the orbiter. The lab is the European Space Agency's contribution to the shuttle program. *(National Aeronautics and Space Administration)*

2

Calculations in the Classroom

The idea grew out of a little classroom exercise, the kind of challenge that teachers lay before their brighter students in hope of exciting their imaginations. But this time, to everyone's surprise—especially the teacher's—the exercise grew into something far beyond anything that might have been expected.

It was the spring of 1969, when many Americans, particularly young people on college campuses, had become deeply disturbed, not only over the U.S. involvement in an unpopular war in Southeast Asia, but also over what was happening at home. Everywhere they looked, in the cities or across the countryside, they saw distressing signs of environmental neglect and decay: mounting piles of garbage and festering tenements, polluted rivers and streams, an atmosphere filled with the deadly fumes of cars and factories, and a landscape scarred with strip mines, recklessly cut forests, and other evidence of exploitation. In addition, despite all appeals for conservation, they found that precious fuel supplies, notably oil and natural gas, were being squandered at an ever-growing rate. Finally, while the United States appeared to be keeping its population within limits, many nations of the developing Third World were growing so rapidly that their needs would inevitably put severe new strains on the world's food and fuel supplies.

At the time, Gerard Kitchen O'Neill, a professor of physics at Princeton University, happened to be giving a course in basic physics. The students, many of whom hoped to become engineers, were quite properly concerned by these serious environmental problems. Indeed, some of them felt that the very technology they were studying in their engineering courses was at the root of much of the trouble. After all, they pointed out, if humans hadn't mastered such dubious skills as oil drilling, strip mining, and other manifestations of contemporary technology, wouldn't Earth be a far more beautiful place without so many difficulties?

O'Neill, to some extent, shared his students' doubts. But he also realized that technology has brought so many benefits that we could not simply abandon it without creating monumental new difficulties; for example, without modern farming techniques requiring chemical fertilizers, large oil-burning machines, and long-haul shipping, much of the world would be plunged into a state of near-starvation. In fact, O'Neill was convinced that technology, although it was often abused, could also be used to ease Earth's environmental problems. Yet how could he convert his students to that idea?

One day he had an inspiration. Gathering together some of the more ambitious students in the physics class, he gave them a special assignment. It would not only relate to their basic concerns about the environment but also show them how technology might be employed for mankind's benefit on a global scale. Quite simply, said O'Neill, he wanted them to begin calculating whether the surface of a planet like Earth was actually the best place to locate an advanced industrial society. Perhaps, in view of all our environmental problems, it might turn out not to be. If that was in fact what their calculations showed, O'Neill added, then he wanted them to propose an alternate site for such an industrial society.

O'Neill, for his part, did not really expect anything extraordinary to come of the students' project. Certainly, it would provide an interesting intellectual test—for the future engineers, in particular. But no matter how imaginative they might be, he felt sure that their calculations would only confirm his own suspicions. Like most of his fellow scientists, O'Neill believed that Earth was, in the words of that fictional optimist Dr. Pangloss, "the best of all possible worlds" for the human race. Space might be exciting for occasional journeys of exploration; in fact, O'Neill had already proposed placing a large, remote-controlled telescope in orbit high above Earth's atmosphere where it could provide a much clearer view of the universe than can terrestrial instruments. But he had never thought seriously about any large exodus from Earth to other parts of the solar system. That was the stuff of science fiction. Humanity's destiny, he believed, was firmly linked to its home planet.

Still, even if they are skeptical about an idea, scientists are often willing to ponder it. No less a physicist than Albert Einstein, who spent the last years of his life only a short distance from O'Neill's office in Princeton, frequently engaged in such "thought" experiments. For example, early in his career he tried to imagine what the world would look like if he were a passenger on a beam of light, traveling at 186,000 miles per second (light's velocity in a vacuum). Einstein recognized the practical impossibility of such a high-speed journey, but merely thinking about the trip helped him realize that an observer moving at a different speed from others nearby sees the universe in a totally different light from the way they do. Though deceptively simple, this concept is at the root of Einstein's revolutionary special theory of relativity, one of the pillars on which twentieth-century science has been built.

O'Neill's objective was hardly so profound. By casting the assignment for his students in global terms, he hoped only to make the calculations a little more "amusing" for them. But, as often happens in science, the questions led to unexpected answers. For instance, in considering the atmosphere, the students discovered that it is one billion times more efficient to hold vital air inside a large cylinder than to retain it by means of gravity, as Earth does. In addition, they found that it is extremely costly in terms of energy to move people and goods across a planetary surface. They calculated that some 25 percent of the energy expended by the U.S. transportation system—about three billion barrels of oil a year—goes toward fighting the pull of Earth's gravity and the resistance of its atmosphere. Says O'Neill: "What began as a joke had to be taken seriously when the numbers began to come out right."

No one was more surprised by those numbers than O'Neill. As a physicist he was intrigued by the large-scale phenomenon of space, but his own special interest was the smaller world of the atom. He had gained particular distinction for his work in particle physics, a branch of physics that studies the tiny, short-lived bits of matter that make up the atom's center, or nucleus.

One of the key methods of probing the nucleus is to break it apart with other speeding particles. For this bash-and-batter technique, particle physicists usually use great doughnut-shaped machines called accelerators, which send particles barreling into fixed target material like well-aimed bullets. Whenever they score a bull's-eye on a nucleus, its fragments are scattered in all directions. If liquid-filled compartments called bubble chambers are placed nearby, the fragments will leave a wake of telltale tracks in the fluid, like footprints in snow. By studying these nuclear footprints, physicists can learn much about the basic structure of matter.

In 1956 O'Neill had proposed a novel improvement in accelerator design. Instead of relying only on a single beam of "bullets" aimed at a stationary target, he suggested using two separate beams. As they moved in opposite directions in the circular accelerator, their paths would occasionally cross. Like two speeding cars careening into each other at an intersection, some of the particles would collide and smash each other to smithereens. The impact at collision would be far greater than that of particles' hitting a fixed nucleus. Impressed by O'Neill's colliding-beam design, scientists have since built such accelerators in a number of countries, including the United States, the Soviet Union, and Switzerland. Already, these new machines, by battering particles harder than ever before, have given physicists valuable new insights into atomic structure.

Important as accelerator development was to him, O'Neill nevertheless found himself increasingly involved in the results of his students' calculations. Again and again, he repeated them, hoping that some flaw could be revealed. But as hard as he tried to discredit the figures, they always came out the same. They pointed to a conclusion that O'Neill would have brushed off as unthinkable a few years earlier: that a small, self-contained colony, whirling through space, could provide humans with virtually all the comforts of life on Earth, and perhaps even more.

No less astounding was the revelation that such a colony was not necessarily a technological daydream. Looking at what it would take to build such a miniworld in space, he realized that preliminary construction could begin almost at once. The means for building the colony were either already available or just within technology's reach.

To make sure he had not erred in some major way, O'Neill took the calculations to his colleagues, hoping they might spot any major flaws—if there were any. But for all his precautions, the answer was always the same: space colonies were an eminently sound idea. Indeed, as he searched the literature of space travel, he found that several far-sighted scientific thinkers had already proposed extraterrestrial colonies, not as escapist fantasy, but as a future technological probability.

One of the earliest proponents of the idea was the Russian space pioneer Konstantin Tsiolkovsky. An obscure, deaf schoolmaster born in the middle of the nineteenth century, he was the first person to carry out serious mathematical studies of the principles of space flight—proposing, among other things, the use of liquid oxygen as rocket fuel long before it was actually burned by moon rockets. In 1895, elaborating on an idea that had already appeared in the writings of the American novelist Edward Everett Hale and the French futurist Jules Verne, Tsiolkovsky mentioned a space station in a science-fiction tale. In fact, he was so sure of the underlying plausibility of the idea that he later provided a detailed description of such a station. His habitat rotated to simulate gravity, made use of solar energy, and had a completely closed ecological system in which wastes were recycled. Wrote Tsiolkovsky: "Earth is the cradle of the mind, but one cannot live in the cradle forever."

Other pioneers followed in Tsiolkovsky's path. As early as 1923, a German rocket theorist, Hermann Oberth, made the suggestion that space stations could be used as platforms for scientific research, including astronomy, and even to observe Earth—an idea that he himself lived to see carried out with the launching of Skylab half a century later. Another writer in the 1920s, Hermann Noordung, actually discussed huge wheels in the sky that could serve as human habitats.

Perhaps the most daring of all these visionaries was the British physicist and science-fiction writer J. D. Bernal. In his imaginative book *The World, the Flesh, and the Devil,* he wrote about completely self-contained little spherical worlds. Beneath their transparent outer skin, they would have food-producing areas that would be bathed in sunlight. Below these would be the machinery that regulated the sphere's temperature and atmosphere. Still lower, in the sphere's hollow central area, would be the colony's major living space. Such worlds, Bernal pointed out, might develop their own cultures and interests. Eventually, perhaps a thousand years from now, so many people might be living in Bernal spheres that only an insignificant part of the human species would still be on Earth or even on other planets in the solar system.

As he pondered such awesome possibilities, O'Neill was increasingly persuaded that they offered a real answer to Earth's problems. By the early 1970s, many scientists already were predicting a planetary doomsday. Computer projections showed that oil, minerals, and other vital resources of industrial societies were being used at such a reckless rate that they would be exhausted early in the twenty-first century. Unless such exploitation could be curbed and the spiraling increase in population halted, said one notable study, *Limits to Growth,* the world faced a global calamity in the not-too-distant future: mass starvation, critical fuel shortages, outbreaks of disease, political upheavals, perhaps even an end to civilization itself.

But O'Neill realized, as had Bernal and others, that space offered an antidote to disaster: an almost unlimited supply of energy from the sun. Soaked in perpetual sunlight, a small colony could tap this resource at will. In contrast, sunlight on Earth is a much more elusive commodity; changing weather conditions that can hide the sun for days, as well as the planet's rotation, which always cloaks part of the planet in darkness, make solar power an unreliable and expensive energy source.

In addition, O'Neill argued, space colonies offered almost endless room for expansion. More and more colonies could be built as long as the mineral supplies of the moon and of other celestial bodies, such as the iron- and carbon-rich asteroids, held out. Meanwhile, the dangerous drain of Earth's own resources could be halted. As the number of people who decided to make new homes for themselves in space increased, industrial pollution and other ecological ravages would decline. Slowly but inevitably, Earth would recover from the assaults of the past. Rivers and the air would become clean again; "dead" lakes would spring back to life. Threatened animal species like the great whales might survive. Indeed, by the middle of the twenty-first century the recovery would have progressed so far that Earth would become, in O'Neill's view, "a worldwide park, a beautiful place to visit for a vacation."

For several frustrating years, O'Neill tried to get scientific journals to publish his ideas. But they seemed far too utopian to his conservative colleagues. Some suggested, not quite fairly, that he was really a frustrated astronaut. (Indeed, a few years earlier O'Neill had been a finalist in NASA's efforts to recruit scientists to its cadre of astronauts, which then consisted largely of former military pilots.) Even those who were willing to concede that humans would eventually settle in space predicted that the colonies would be established on planetary surfaces, like that of the moon, not as self-sufficient habitats in free space. Repeatedly, in spite of O'Neill's impressive credentials as a physicist, the journals refused to print his proposals.

At the suggestion of sympathetic friends, he decided to take his cause directly "to the people." Many scientists frown on this tactic; they believe that scientific ideas should first be evaluated within the confines of the scientific community. But despite the professional risks it entailed, O'Neill began talking about space colonization in public lectures at college and universities. The response exceeded his wildest expectations. Especially among students, he found the proposal welcomed with unabashed enthusiasm. In fact, their provocative questions stimulated O'Neill himself to look more deeply into space colonies. Could they survive a meteoroid hit, for example? What kind of food would the colonists eat? The answers only fortified his own, and many of his listeners', faith in the idea.

By 1974 O'Neill had managed to stage the first formal conferences on space colonization. He had become such a persuasive advocate that even sober-minded officials of NASA showed up at Princeton for the meeting, in spite of the possible scorn they faced from their colleagues. O'Neill, whose butcher-boy hair style makes him look vaguely like Mr. Spock of the *Star Trek* television series, wryly acknowledged their appearance: "It's a tribute to their bravery, I think, that they are willing even to be seen here." Shortly thereafter, the prestigious journal *Physics Today*, overcoming initial reluctance, agreed to publish a paper by O'Neill outlining his scheme. Space colonization was finally getting the serious consideration that it deserved.

One of those who listened attentively to O'Neill's ideas was a

Dr. Gerard K. O'Neill, space colonization's gifted advocate, cheerfully contemplates the good life in space as he explains an artist's conception of a Bernal sphere-type space habitat. *(Frederic Golden)*

fellow physicist, Freeman Dyson of the neighboring Institute for Advanced Study in Princeton. He had special reason to be interested. A gifted theorist, he had already peered into the future and speculated that advanced civilizations, in their hunger for energy, might encircle the sun with a huge sphere of space habitats. In that way, they would be able to trap much more of the sun's radiation. To astronomers on planets orbiting a distant star, the rather ordinary, middle-aged celestial object that is our sun would no longer be visible, but its halo of habitats would be detectable by their own heat or infrared radiation. Dyson thus encouraged O'Neill to look further into the concept of space colonization, although he admitted that he personally might find life a little confining and sterile in his colleague's orbital worlds.

The publicity made O'Neill something of a celebrity. Handsome, quietly articulate, he was asked to speak about his colonies on radio and television, to write additional articles, and even to testify before a Congressional subcommittee on space. Meanwhile, around the country, his enthusiastic supporters were forming a citizens' group named the L5 Society, after the location in space where he thinks the first colony should be built. Chapters of the society sprouted in several cities; one even began in Britain. The members included not only science-fiction buffs but many young scientists and engineers as well.

In 1975 an even larger conference was held at Princeton. This time O'Neill was able to gather more than a hundred specialists, including, in addition to space scientists and engineers, agricultural experts, political scientists, architects, and even an expert on international law. Though they represented widely different disciplines, the participants agreed that, whatever difficulties space colonization entailed, they could be overcome. A few months later, the idea received an even more ringing endorsement.

For ten weeks, twenty-eight experts, including O'Neill himself, met under the joint auspices of NASA's Ames Research

Center near San Francisco and Stanford University to evaluate space colonization. It was the most penetrating examination yet made of O'Neill's blueprint for the future. Some of the experts disagreed on the details of colonization and warned that it might be more costly than O'Neill's original estimate—he had said that the first colony would not cost much more than the Apollo program. But after the summer-long study, they not only concluded that space colonization was feasible but urged the United States to begin such a program.

Equally important, the multi-discipline team reaffirmed the essential value of the idea by also examining a new feature: the use of space colonies and materials mined on the moon to construct solar power stations that could provide Earth with electricity. Even if such electricity were sold at bargain-basement rates, the money that was collected could easily pay for the colonies and the lunar mining camps. The following summer another study group was convened at Ames, with O'Neill again participating. It explored in considerable detail how the lunar material could be launched to the colonies and how it could be chemically processed into usable building blocks.

Meanwhile, despite a certain amount of understandable skepticism, officials in Washington were beginning to take increasing note of the Princeton professor's seemingly far-fetched proposal. O'Neill was called to make personal presentations not only to NASA's top brass, which had initially disdained his scheme but now promised more funds for further studies, but also to Congressional committees concerned with the future of the U.S. role in space. Clearly, the idea of space colonization was beginning to take root.

If the program that was born in a Princeton classroom did in fact succeed, it would be mankind's boldest step yet. In the words of the 1975 summer group, it would be comparable "to the transition of life from the sea to the land or the transition of our progenitors from life in the primitive forests to the open plains."

An aerial photograph of NASA's Ames Research Center in Californiá *(right of center)*, site of much of the preliminary scientific discussion on the possibility of building permanent habitats in space. *(National Aeronautics and Space Administration)*

3

Dreamers and Prophets

No one can really say how long man has been dreaming about space travel. But it is one of those timeless fantasies found in the myths and legends of many cultures.

More than 4,000 years ago the ancient Egyptians buried their dead pharaohs with a replica of the royal barge, not only as an act of homage to the god-king but also to ensure his successful ascent to heaven. The Bible also tells of such journeys. At the end of his earthly days, the prophet Elijah "went up by a whirlwind into heaven." There is even an Old Testament vision of Unidentified Flying Objects (UFOs). In the story of Ezekiel, a mysterious craft appears out the sky and lands near a river in Chaldea, part of ancient Babylonia.

To the ancients, space (or heaven) was the home of the gods. All important heavenly bodies were linked with deities—especially the so-called wandering stars, or planets, which appeared to move back and forth across a celestial belt called the zodiac. The brightest of these objects in the nighttime sky except for the moon was the planet Venus, which was identified with the goddess of love. The most rapidly moving of the planets was Mercury, the fleet-footed messenger of the gods. Mars, whose reddish, bloodlike color gave it an awesome look, was the god of war. Saturn reigned over agriculture. Jupiter was named for the supreme god. Though the ancients did not realize it, their choice was appropriate: Jupiter is the solar system's largest planet, a body more than three hundred times as massive as Earth.

In ancient eyes, challenging the gods could be perilous business. This was something that two celebrated mythical characters quickly learned. Determined to attempt a voyage beyond Earth, Daedalus and his son Icarus made themselves birdlike wings out of feathers and wax and took off. But young Icarus was not content. Against his father's advice, he flew recklessly close to the sun. Its heat promptly melted the wax of his wings, and Icarus plunged to his death in the sea.

Greek storytellers, who were the entertainers of their day, did not really expect their listeners to accept this tale as literal truth. But there was nevertheless a lesson for everyone in Icarus's fate. By Greek standards, he had committed an unforgivable sin. In thinking that he could reach the sun, he was displaying the exaggerated, overreaching pride that the Greeks called *hubris;* any mortal who mocked the gods in this way risked their retribution. In short, the story was intended as a warning to those who would dare to venture into the unknown.

That ancient message has its modern echo in the preachings of those critics of scientific progress who gloomily speak out against any bold new undertaking—whether it is a radical new research program or a rocket trip to the moon. But well-intentioned as such advice may be, it ignores a fundamental impulse that distinguishes humans from virtually all other creatures: the irresistible urge to explore and understand the world about them.

The earliest-known work of science fiction dealing with space travel dates back to the second century A.D. when the

Greek writer Lucian of Samosata produced his humorously titled *True History*. In fact, it is utter fantasy. It is about a hero who sails beyond the Pillars of Hercules into a vast, unknown region of ocean, where his ship is suddenly lifted by a giant waterspout and carried all the way to the moon. Later, on a second voyage, Lucian's hero actually manages to fly to the moon with a pair of Icarus-type wings.

Lucian's choice of the moon for an extraterrestrial landing is not really surprising. Even in his day, long before the invention of the telescope, anyone could see that the moon was a sphere and that it had curious markings; in a vague way, these suggested an earthlike landscape. By using trigonometric techniques, the ancients also determined how far away the moon was. In fact, about 130 B.C., the astronomer Hipparchus of Nicaea correctly calculated that it was about thirty Earth diameters distant. That meant that the moon, to appear as large as it does over such a distance (240,000 miles), had to have a girth at least a sizable fraction of Earth's. All in all, it even seemed possible to some ancient stargazers that the moon might be inhabited.

For a long time after Lucian's imaginative *History,* all thoughts of space were forgotten. Europe slumbered for many centuries; scientific speculation virtually ceased. But by the sixteenth century there were signs of a reawakening. After years of cautious work, a Polish churchman-astronomer named Nicolaus Copernicus wrote a slim little book called *On the Revolutions of the Heavenly Orbs* (published in 1543). Copernicus's volume was indeed revolutionary. Arguing against prevailing wisdom, he said that the sun, not Earth, occupied the central position in the universe. Earth, in his view, was just one of the sun's family of planets.

It was a bold, even a dangerous concept. By demoting Earth, Copernicus was also indirectly making man a little less important; religious ideas then suggested that man, a creature made in God's image, had to be unique. But if Earth was only one of

This old print shows Nicolaus Copernicus clutching a tiny representation of the sun. Copernicus upset sixteenth-century doctrine by claiming that the sun, not Earth, occupied the central position in the universe. (*The New York Public Library Picture Collection*)

several planets circling the sun, it could not really be very different from these bodies; possibly they were inhabited too. The fiery Dominican monk Giordano Bruno proposed a more fantastical idea. "Innumerable suns exist," he insisted. "Innumerable Earths revolve about these suns. . . . Living things inhabit these worlds." Bruno's heretical talk so frightened church authorities that they burned him at the stake.

But as theologically unsettling as the new Copernican universe may have been, even its opponents eventually had to accept it as fact. Nothing did more to settle the argument than the accidental invention of the telescope by an obscure lens grinder in Holland in 1608. By the following year, the great Italian scientist Galileo Galilei had made his own crude telescope and turned it toward the heavens. Though it was no better than a pair of cheap present-day binoculars, Galileo's "optick stick" opened up a whole new universe.

Looking at the planet Jupiter, he was astounded to find that it was itself surrounded by four little moons. In effect, here was another little solar system; the Jovian moons were orbiting Jupiter, just as Earth and the other planets were circling the sun. He also saw that Venus was a bright crescent; it waxed and waned like the moon, a hint that it shone by reflected light from the sun. But the discovery that most impressed everyone was that of the appearance of the moon. It was not a smooth sphere but covered with what seemed to be many mountains, valleys, and even seas (a mistake that is still perpetuated today in the word *mare,* or sea, to describe parts of the lunar surface). To Galileo, this distant world was "the most beautiful and delightful sight."

Galileo's studies marked the beginnings of modern observational astronomy. No longer could anyone realistically argue, as had the ancient Greeks, that the planets and stars were imbedded in rotating crystal spheres, nestling inside of one another like a set of glass salad bowls. The observations also shattered the medieval idea that the universe was a three-tiered cosmos consisting of heaven, Earth, and hell. Thanks to the telescope, scientists could see not only farther into space, but also more clearly. The heavens became less a subject of speculation by theologians and poets than an object of serious investigation by scientific-minded stargazers.

One of this new breed of astronomers was Galileo's German contemporary Johannes Kepler, who discovered the laws of planetary motion. These are nature's inflexible rules that determine the motion of celestial bodies down to the smallest spacecraft in orbit round Earth. In fact, it was Kepler who coined the word that we still use today to describe such captive

A painting by Gatti portrays the great Italian scientist Galileo Galilei at a Florentine court. *(The Bettmann Archive)*

bodies. Discussing the moons of Jupiter, he dubbed them "satellites," from the Latin word that the Romans applied to the followers of wealthy men who constantly hover around them in hopes of getting special favors.

Kepler also used his literary talents to write an amusing fable called *Somnium* (Sleep) about a trip to the moon. Unlike Lucian, he knew that there was no atmosphere between Earth and the moon to support winged creatures; atmospheric resistance would have long since slowed the planets down so much that they would have crashed into the sun. But still he had to get his travelers to the moon. Too good a scientist to resort to wings or waterspouts, he wrote his story in the form of a dream in which spirits carried them to the moon. Actually, considering the times in which he lived, it was not so fantastical an idea. Kepler's own mother had been accused of witchcraft. But in other ways Kepler's dream has the ring of truth. His lunar inhabitants, for example, are tough-skinned creatures who hide from the strong sun in caves. He correctly described the lunar day and night, each of which is two weeks long. He was also far ahead of his time in his description of what it feels like to be launched into space. "Initial movement is most uncomfortable and dangerous," he wrote, "for the traveler is torn aloft as if blown by gunpowder." Even more incredible, he accurately foresaw that his astronauts would experience "bitter cold and lack of air to breathe" and lose all sense of weight. Indeed, Kepler marshaled scientific facts so well that many scholars regard his tale as the first real work of science fiction, as opposed to Lucian's science fantasy.

Unfortunately, the foresighted Kepler did not live to get any acclaim for his tale; it was published in 1634, a year after his death. But the literary form he created soon produced imitators. A year later, the English clergyman Francis Godwin published *Man in the Moone,* the first sci-fi tale of a lunar voyage written in English. Godwin's hero, a Spaniard named Domingo Gonsales, hitches a chariot to some swans. To his astonishment, they carry him off to the moon, where he finds a pleasant land that resembles newly discovered America. While Godwin's story was much less scientific than Kepler's, he did correctly anticipate a still-unknown gravitational feature of the moon. His hero found that he weighed much less on the moon and could jump far higher than on Earth.

Of all the authors to write about space travel in those days, none could match the ingenuity and wit of the Frenchman Cyrano de Bergerac. A duelist, adventurer, and man of letters, the long-nosed Cyrano (who has since been immortalized on stage and film) wrote as flamboyantly as he lived. His book *Voyage to the Moon and Sun*, published in 1656, describes a number of methods of flight that are uncannily modern. For the first time in science fiction, a space traveler makes use of a rocket. Cyrano also dreamed up a machine with wings and propeller that seems to foreshadow the airplane. Another of his spacecraft is even more advanced. At one end of his fictional ship, hot gases are expelled, while at the other end gases from space rush in to fill the void, thereby creating enough suction to pull the spacecraft in that direction. Cyrano, of course, had his basic physics confused, but his hot-air machine comes close to predicting today's jet engine.

Ingenious as their schemes may have been, would-be space travelers soon had to cope with a new reality. In 1687 Britain's Sir Isaac Newton published his monumental *Principia* (pronounced *prin-KIP-ee-uh*), the full Latin title of which is *Philosophiae Naturalis Principia Mathematica* (The Mathematical Principles of Natural Philosophy). Perhaps the greatest single scientific work of all time, it set forth the laws of motion and universal gravitation. Extending its reach throughout the universe, Newton's gravity governed the movements of all objects— from the fall of the legendary apple, which is said to have started Newton thinking about gravity, to the orbits of planets and other objects in space. No one could hope to defy these inviolable rules. They were so precise and calculable that the solar system's components seemed to move like the finely machined parts of a giant clockwork. If there was the slightest deviation in a celestial body's movements, it had to have a cause. For example, astronomers looking for what was pulling Uranus off course discovered the planet Neptune.

In Newton's universe, gravity reigned supreme. If any astronauts wanted to escape Earth's—or any other planet's—gravitational grasp, Newton's laws dictated that their ship had to reach a speed precisely dependent on the body's mass. In the case of a planet as large as Earth, this turned out to be many thousands of miles per hour. No cannon ball or bullet in Newton's day (or even in ours) could reach such velocities; the necessary speed would not be attained until the development of sophisticated chemical rockets in the twentieth century. But the technological shortcomings of his era did not keep Newton from making calculations for projectiles in space.

He reckoned that if a projectile could somehow be fired horizontally off into space from atop a high mountain at some 8 kilometers (5 miles) per second or nearly 29,000 kilometers (18,000 miles) per hour—what we now call orbital velocity—it would not fall back to the ground but continue to whirl around Earth indefinitely. If the projectile's speed could be boosted to, say, about 11 kilometers (7 miles) per second or nearly 40,000 kilometers (25,000 miles) per hour, it would reach escape velocity. That is, it would break out of orbit and soar off into deep space.

While even the genius of Newton did not foresee how such great speeds would be achieved, he was instrumental in another way. It has long been clear that only rocket ships could travel across the near-vacuum of space; by contrast, the air-breathing engines of jets would sputter to a halt if the aircraft tried to climb beyond the lower atmosphere. But rockets carry all their own propellants, including oxygen, so they do not depend on their environment. When these propellants—which can be solid or liquid chemicals—are ignited, they expel hot gases at high velocity from one end of the rocket and push the ship in the opposite direction. But how? Obviously, in the chilly void of space, there is nothing to push against, yet somehow the rocket manages to reach tremendous speeds. The answer lies in Newton's famous Third Law of Motion: "For every action there is an equal and opposite reaction."

It sounds simple, but the law is deceptive and still sometimes misunderstood. Even in our own day, people often find it difficult to explain how a rocket works. One notorious example of such misunderstanding was an editorial that appeared in the *New York Times* in 1921, scoffing at the dream of the American rocket pioneer Robert Hutchings Goddard to fire rockets at the moon. Didn't the professor know, the editorial writer jeeringly asked, that a rocket had "to have something better than a vacuum against which to react . . . knowledge ladled out daily in high schools?" Nearly half a century later, though Goddard by then was dead, the *Times,* to its credit, apologized in another editorial about him on the occasion of the first moon landing.

In any case, one doesn't need to travel to the moon by rocket to see the truth in Newton's law. One familiar example of the principle of action and reaction is the recoil that occurs when a rifle is fired. As the bullet barrels out of the gun, it kicks the rifle's stock in the opposite direction against the gunner's shoulder. Another example sometimes takes place when a novice tries to ride a skateboard. If the rider tumbles off in one direction, the skateboard inevitably will shoot off in the other. Painful as it may be, such a mishap can be a perfect display of Newton's Third Law in action.

Newton, however, did more than work out the theory of errant skateboards or space-age rockets. By showing that all the planets in the solar system had to obey the same set of universal laws, he gave added credence to another popular notion: that they were also all inhabited. The great scientist himself believed this; he even speculated that there might be life on the sun. According to one idea of the time, the intelligence of planetary beings increased directly in proportion to their distance from the sun. Thus, by this mathematical reckoning, Martians, dwelling on the fourth planet from the sun, were considerably brighter than the inhabitants of the third, Earth.

In 1752 the French philosopher Voltaire went so far as to imagine life far beyond the solar system. In *Micromegas*, he describes the visit to Earth by a giant from a planet in the vicinity of the bright star Sirius, along with a companion from Saturn. The extraterrestrial twosome observe the strange behavior of Earthlings, especially that of scientists, writers, politicians, and others whom Voltaire wanted to ridicule. Like other satirists before and after him, Voltaire used science-fiction themes as a convenient vehicle to poke fun at human foibles.

Europeans were not the only people to enjoy such tales. In 1835 the *New York Sun* greatly boosted circulation by running a series of mock-serious stories about life on the moon. The American author Edgar Allan Poe showed his skills at science fiction with a story titled "The Unparalleled Adventure of One Hans Pfaal." Using a balloon filled with a mysterious gas, Poe's hero travels all the way to the moon. By then, balloons had already lifted men to considerable heights, but even the lightest gas, hydrogen, could not have taken a balloonist above the atmosphere. In 1870 the Boston clergyman-author Edward Everett Hale published a more scientifically perceptive tale. Called "The Brick Moon," it concerns orbiting a large sphere above Earth as a navigational aid to mariners at sea, an idea that anticipates the satellites launched less than a century later.

As it happens, Hale's orbiter accidentally became the first modern colony in space. Some two hundred feet in diameter and made of bricks because Hale thought they were the best material for resisting the frictional heat of a fast ride through the atmosphere, the artificial moon was to be hurled into space by a spinning flywheel. But somehow it rolled onto this catapult a bit too early, while many workers were still inside the satellite. So off they went into orbit with it. Luckily, they had plenty of food and supplies aboard their brick moon, including egg-laying hens (birds that would later be advocated for real-life space colonists as a protein source). Making the best of their little world, they continued to live in space and kept Earth abreast of their activities by a kind of makeshift signaling system from the exterior of their brick space colony.

But one nineteenth-century writer did more than any other to stir fantasies about traveling in space. In 1865 the Frenchman Jules Verne published *From the Earth to the Moon,* describing a lunar trip by several Americans inside a large cannon shell. Verne was such a stickler for scientific accuracy that he had his astronomer brother-in-law calculate the precise velocities. More remarkable, Verne's astronauts were launched from Florida, only a short distance from the place where real Americans were to start their moon trip a century later.

Verne conveniently neglected to explain how his travelers survived the cannon's initial concussion or the tremendous gravitational forces (g's) that would have built up in their capsule. But in other respects his entertaining tale was more scientifically rigorous. For example, he equipped the ship with small steering rockets; thus he anticipated the small thrusters used today to make course corrections on space flights. Shrewdly, Verne did not land his astronauts on the moon's surface. In that way he avoided the problem of getting them off the moon. Instead, like America's Apollo 8 astronauts, who made the first trip to the moon, Verne's spacemen circled around it and used lunar gravity to help kick them back to Earth.

These were not Verne's only modern touches. Before embarking on their journey, his astronauts first tested their scheme by sending up a cat and squirrel in a hollow shell; thus he anticipated the biomedical launches of our day. Unfortunately, the test was only partially successful: during the flight the cat ate the squirrel.

Verne was so popular that he also produced many imitators. But only one was his equal—the English writer H. G. Wells. In

1901 Wells published *The First Men in the Moon*. As his means of propulsion, he had the spacecraft for the lunar flight entirely covered with a mysterious anti-gravity substance called "Cavorite." All his spacemen had to do was to uncover a small porthole in the moon's direction, and lunar gravity would tug on the exposed part and pull the ship toward the moon.

Later Wells wrote his epic *The War of the Worlds*. Still popular today, it describes an attack by Martians against Earth. Only when the three-legged invaders finally succumb to terrestrial bacteria is the planet saved. The plot did not seem entirely farfetched to many readers. At the time, the early-twentieth-century American astronomer Percival Lowell was

These nineteenth-century drawings illustrated an early edition of Jules Verne's *From the Earth to the Moon*. Verne described the launching of a large cannon shell (containing several intrepid American space travelers) from the Florida peninsula to the moon.

insisting that the markings he saw on the Martian surface were in fact artificial canals dug out by the intelligent inhabitants to tap water for their dying civilization from the icy polar regions. The recent reconnaissance of Mars by unmanned Mariner spacecraft shows that Lowell's canals are apparently wind-carved features in the dusty Martian surface.

But many Americans still remember that famous Halloween night in 1938 when the actor Orson Welles broadcast a dramatization of *The War of the Worlds*. It was done so realistically that many listeners actually believed that what they heard was really happening, and panic broke out in the streets.

Looking back upon them in the light of all of today's

achievements in space, the efforts of H. G. Wells, Verne, and other pioneers of space literature may seem unbelievably naive. But to laugh them off entirely would be a serious injustice. As musty as they may now seem, in their day they had an enormous impact on the minds of their audiences.

One youngster who read Verne was Massachusetts-born Robert Goddard, who even as a teen-ager thought seriously of rockets and interplanetary flights. In 1926, while he was still a relatively obscure physics teacher at Clark University in Worcester, Massachusetts, he fired the world's first successful liquid-fueled rocket. His missile reached a height of only 184 feet, but Goddard's noisy backyard experiments on his Aunt Effie's farm so frightened her Massachusetts neighbors that he was soon forced to conduct his pioneering rocketry elsewhere, first on a desolate U.S. Army artillery range, then in the desert near Roswell, New Mexico. Because he was sure that such researches would eventually lead to flights to the moon and other planets and didn't hesitate to say so publicly, he left himself open to a certain amount of scorn. After one of Goddard's rocket firings in 1929, a newspaper headline sneered: "Moon Rocket Misses Target by 238,799 1/2 miles."

As a young man, Goddard had proposed an even bolder flight plan for future rockets. In 1918 he wrote about the possibility of a huge spaceship, a kind of Noah's Ark, which could carry the remnants of an entire civilization from a dying solar system to start life anew in orbit around another star. Goddard even suggested that the ark–spaceship might be propelled by nuclear power; at the time this was no more than a dim mathematical possibility. But perhaps because he thought he might look like a hopeless dreamer in the eyes of his hard-headed colleagues, he hid away the manuscript (aptly titled "The Ultimate Migration"). It did not come to light again until half a century later when his widow, Esther, allowed publication of his papers.

Another giant of the space age who read Verne as a

youngster and was inspired by his writings was Konstantin Tsiolkovsky. Living in the countryside near Moscow at the turn of the century, Tsiolkovsky became obsessed with space flight. Largely self-taught in physics and mathematics, he poured out a remarkable number of technical and popular papers on rocketry. Many of them turned out to be uncannily accurate. In 1903, for example, while the Wright brothers were barely getting off the ground at Kitty Hawk, he described how a manned space station could be rotated to simulate gravity. He also dressed his space travelers in "ether suits" that were virtually blueprints for today's pressurized space garb. In addition, he let them mine the riches of the asteroids. He was even so bold as to predict that humans would populate the entire solar system.

Tsiolkovsky was luckier than Goddard. He was not shunned or ridiculed by his countrymen. On the contrary, his writings were widely distributed in the Soviet Union in the 1920s and 1930s, and in the last years of his long life the one-time schoolteacher was a national hero. Though few people outside Russia had heard of him, Tsiolkovsky was given a state funeral when he died in 1935. In light of this long Russian interest in rocketry, Westerners—especially Americans—should not have been surprised when the Soviet Union turned Tsiolkovsky's dream into reality in 1957 by successfully launching Sputnik 1, the world's first artificial satellite.

Tsiolkovsky and Goddard were perhaps the most celebrated figures of the space age to get their inspiration from Verne and his fellow science-fiction writers. But those imaginative writings also stirred the minds of countless other young readers, many of whom went on to become leading scientists and engineers in the space program. Perhaps mankind would eventually have sent rockets into space or reached the moon even if there had never been a Verne or an H. G. Wells or a Cyrano, but certainly we would not have done it so soon—or enjoyed it so much—without the urging of their bold dreams and prophecies.

4

Eighty-four Days Around the World

It was a balmy spring day in May 1973 when the giant thirty-five-story Saturn 5 rocket lifted off from Florida's Kennedy Space Center. Spewing flames and shaking the ground for miles around, the big booster roared skyward until it was lost in the clouds. But as spectacular as the launch was, it attracted curiously little public attention.

There were no blaring headlines before the blast-off. Television provided only routine coverage. Four years earlier, in July 1969, when a similar Saturn 5 rocketed off with three men bound for the first landing on the moon, at least a million people had thronged to watch the awesome moment from the nearby beaches of Cape Canaveral. Many millions more—perhaps even a billion—watched the historic launch on TV. Now, as the latest

Saturn began its journey, onlookers at the cape numbered only in the thousands.

Veteran observers of the space program did not have to search hard for an explanation of this public indifference. By 1973 many Americans had become quite blasé about space travel. Twelve men had already walked on the dusty lunar surface. Except for one disaster on the launch pad, when three men were killed by fire, and another near-disaster in space, when an oxygen tank exploded aboard Apollo 13, the lunar missions had been executed so flawlessly that they seemed drained of all drama and excitement. In addition, as interesting as the lunar rocks and scientific data gathered on the moon may have been to researchers, many people wondered whether this specialized knowledge was worth the cost of the $24 billion Apollo program.

Against this background of public doubt and hostility, the Saturn 5 raced into the sky. Even though the launch attracted far less notice than any of the moon shots, it was at least as important—perhaps even more so. For the first time the United States was attempting to put into Earth orbit an experimental space station, Skylab, in which astronauts would live and work for a duration much longer than the ten-day trips to the moon.

As Skylab circled Earth at an altitude of 430 kilometers (270 miles), three astronauts—Charles ("Pete") Conrad, a veteran of Apollo 12; Paul Weitz; and Joseph Kerwin, the first medical doctor in space—stood by at the Kennedy Space Center, waiting to follow the station into orbit the next day. Slated to remain aboard for twenty-eight days, they would attempt to set a new longevity record for space flights. When they completed their mission, two more teams of astronauts would board Skylab for even longer stays.

Looking like a squat grain silo, Skylab was admirably suited for such assignments. Its interior contained as much space as a three-bedroom house; in contrast, the Apollo command ships that took the astronauts to the moon had about as much room as a minibus. To provide Skylab's large accommodations, space planners emptied out the Saturn's third-stage booster (which was needed on moon flights to kick the Apollo astronauts out of Earth orbit and send them hurtling toward the moon) and replaced its fuel tanks and plumbing with almost all the comforts of home: sleeping facilities for each of the astronauts, a kitchen, an exercising area, a zero-g toilet (instead of Apollo's crude plumbing), a little library, a tape recorder, and even a dart board. In addition, the laboratory was stocked with enough scientific gear to be the envy of any earthbound scientist. Nothing quite like it had ever been seen before in space. The Russians had orbited smaller, simpler *Salyut* space stations. By contrast, Skylab was so large and so well equipped that it looked like a setting from the futuristic film *2001*.

Space officials had gone to such great lengths in building Skylab in order to answer some important questions. They knew that humans could survive brief missions to the moon. In fact, in preparing for the lunar program, astronauts had spent two weeks or more in orbit aboard smaller Gemini spacecraft. But could the human body cope with longer periods of weightlessness without damaging, say, the muscles or the cardiovascular system? Already, space doctors had detected some disturbing losses of calcium in the bones after some missions. Before anyone could even begin to think about more ambitious projects—a year-long journey to Mars, for instance, or even the establishment of space colonies, which would require workers to spend considerable time in zero-g—NASA had to know the body's endurance limits.

The space agency realized that there would be no better way to find out than by letting astronauts perform useful scientific work in space. Among Skylab's scheduled experiments were a number that had been suggested by high-school youngsters in a national competititon. One teen-ager wanted the astronauts to search for ultraviolet emissions from pulsars, which are the compressed remains of dying stars. Another asked them to look at heat emissions from inactive volcanoes to see if they were about to erupt. The experiment that especially caught the public's fancy involved two spiders named Anita and Arabella. The astronauts would carry them into space to see if they could spin normal webs in weightlessness.

Besides these activities suggested by the youngsters, the astronauts would also spend considerable time making observations of the sun with their multimillion-dollar solar telescope. From its position above the atmosphere, this instrument would be able to watch the sun far more closely than could astronomers with telescopes on Earth. Perhaps it would provide new clues to such puzzles as the sun's effects on Earth's weather, climate, and even radio communications.

From their 430-kilometer- (270-mile) high perch, the astronauts would be able to observe not only the heavens but also Earth. Such monitoring from space could be useful in unexpected ways. Even during the briefer Gemini and Apollo flights, orbital photography of Earth revealed important information about crop and forest conditions, cloud cover, and the location of mineral deposits. Now they would have access to a wider variety of cameras and film and be able to make a far more intense reconnaissance of Earth. An equally important scientific activity aboard Skylab would involve testing such precision manufacturing processes as the casting of ball bearings, the growth of crystals for electronic components, and the separation of chemicals for drugs and antibiotics. On Earth, all these processes are affected by gravity; ball bearings, for instance, turn out to be slightly less than perfect spheres because of it. If the astronomers could show that such operations could be carried out better in zero-g, the results would provide a powerful incentive for another human activity in space: the establishment of zero-g factories.

High as were the hopes of its planners for the mission's success, they soon had every reason for gloom. The big rocket had barely cleared its tower when automatic signals from Skylab indicated serious trouble. By the time the eighty-five-ton spaceship settled into orbit, mission controllers realized that the stresses and vibrations of the launch had ripped off a thin but crucial shielding, an external wrapping that was to act as both a sunshade and a protector against micro-meteoroids and cosmic rays. The ship's interior was already overheating—threatening not only delicate scientific instruments and film but also food supplies and other perishables for the astronauts. But heat was not the only problem. When the shielding tore off, it took along with it one of Skylab's electricity-generating solar wings and prevented another from extending. Without these panels the laboratory's electricity supply would be cut to less than half of the wattage required for full operation.

To the space agency's chagrin, it looked almost as if the $2.5 billion mission had flopped completely even before any astronauts set foot aboard Skylab. But NASA's resourceful scientists and engineers are a "never say die" group; during the worst moments of the Apollo 13 mission, they coolly devised a makeshift means of getting the endangered astronauts safely back to Earth. In effect, they used the little lunar lander, which was still linked to the command module, as a life raft. They let the lander's oxygen and electricity replace that which was not available from the mother ship, whose systems had been battered by the explosion of an oxygen tank. Now, while Conrad, Weitz, and Kerwin waited anxiously on the ground, the engineers' ingenuity was again being tested. As a first step, they fired Skylab's little thruster rockets, changing its position so that less sunlight beat down on the exposed area where the shielding had ripped off. Almost immediately temperatures inside went down—to about 38 degrees Celsius (100 degrees Fahrenheit). That drop would protect the ship from further damage, but it was still too hot for humans to live on board.

In round-the-clock consultations among officials at Houston, Cape Canaveral, and Huntsville, Alabama, where Skylab had

The battered but highly successful Skylab space station circling Earth, as seen from above by the last team of astronauts during a final inspection before their return home. The ship has only one solar "wing" and is covered by a makeshift shielding that was deployed in space by the astronauts themselves. *(National Aeronautics and Space Administration)*

Eighty-four Days Around the World   59

been assembled, the space agency settled on a daring solution. To protect Skylab's "bald spot," the astronauts would be asked to fasten a thin plastic awning over the outside of the ship. It would be a space-age first: an orbital repair 435 kilometers (270 miles) above Earth. If it worked, it would add enormous weight to the argument that astronauts could attempt even more ambitious construction projects in space.

Eleven days after Skylab's troubled launch, the three crew members finally took off after their stricken home in orbit. After several passes around Earth, they caught up with Skylab and gingerly approached it. Leaning out of the hatch of his Apollo commandship, Weitz tried furiously to free the jammed solar wing by poking it with a long pole that had a cutting tool at its far end. But the wing stubbornly refused to budge. It was jammed by a small bit of metal—"One lousy bolt," muttered Conrad.

Nonetheless, the astronauts docked with Skylab and entered the workshop. Next day they donned their pressure suits, opened a small hatch, and managed to cover enough of Skylab's exposed skin to bring down temperatures to a comfortable level almost immediately. But that didn't solve all their problems. Unless the ship's electrical supply could be boosted, their activities, including some of the important experiments, would have to be drastically curtailed. The two follow-up Skylab missions might have to be canceled altogether.

Refusing to give up, Conrad and Weitz climbed outside the ship a few days later and again tackled the balky solar wing. Tugging and pushing so furiously that even controllers down in Houston heard some of their radioed cussing, they eventually pried loose the jamming metal, and the wing immediately popped into place. Thanks to this display of old-fashioned Yankee ingenuity in the new environment of space, the mission was saved. The astronauts went on to spend a record twenty-eight days in orbit. When they finally returned, they brought with them no fewer than 30,000 pictures of the sun, to say nothing of the piles of other scientific data.

But even this achievement was soon to be outshone; the second Skylab team spent fifty-nine days in space, roughly two months' travel time away from their home planet. The trio—Alan Bean, Jack Lousma, and Owen Garriot—took more than 100,000 pictures of the sun, Earth, and stars. They recorded so much data that they used up eighteen miles of magnetic tape, and they spent several hours outside Skylab erecting another sunshade. As a result of an improved exercise program, they were in even better shape when they came home than the Skylab 1 team had been. Only the spiders were casualties, although Arabella did manage to spin a perfectly normal web in zero-g before she died.

Eventually Skylab 2's record was also eclipsed. Skylab 3 astronauts Gerald Carr, William Pogue, and Edward Gibson spent an extraordinary eighty-four days above Earth. In spite of some nausea at the outset of their mission and a slight loss of red blood cells, they were exceptionally fit upon their return; Gibson even started jogging immediately. NASA's doctors credited their good condition to their dedicated exercise with the lab's bicycle and treadmill. Less rigorous but more playful activities in Skylab's environs may also have helped; Carr, for one, would open a jar of peanuts, let them drift away, then "swim" after them with his mouth open and try to gulp them down like a hungry guppy.

Skylab's great success, especially after its nearly disastrous beginning, enormously boosted NASA's confidence in the future of the manned space effort. Before Skylab, many officials were quietly skeptical about the ability of humans to spend long periods in space. Even if they survived physically, it was argued, they would eventually break down from extreme loneliness and isolation. Skylab indicated that this was not so; aside from gathering enormous quantities of scientific data, the nine Skylab

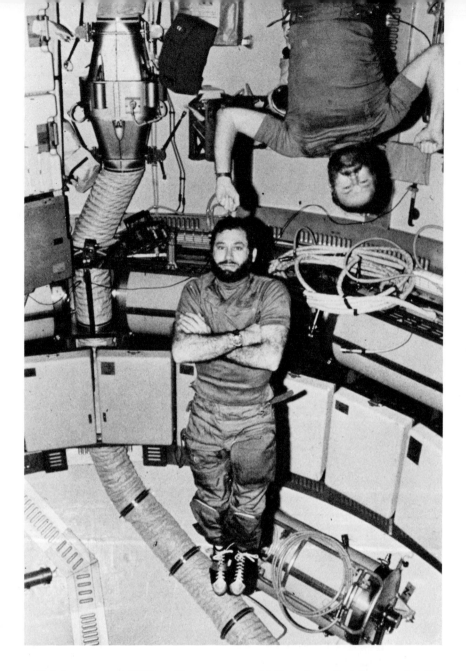

Skylab astronauts William Pogue and Gerald Carr show that they are totally indifferent to weight in a picture taken by their fellow crewman Edward Gibson during their record eighty-four days in orbit. (*National Aeronautics and Space Administration*)

astronauts showed that humans could make a home for themselves in space without suffering debilitating physical or psychological damage.

Such reassurances were highly welcome to the space agency. Without them it would be pointless even to discuss bolder adventures like the establishment of a space colony.

Astronaut Jack Lousma enjoys a refreshing shower aboard Skylab during his fifty-nine days in orbit. *(National Aeronautics and Space Administration)*

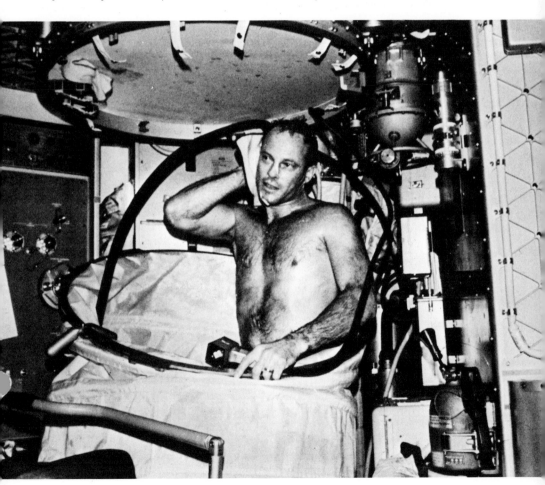

5

Mining on the Moon

From a distance of a quarter of a million miles, it looms beckoningly in the night sky. But attractive as the moon may seem from Earth, it is an extremely inhospitable world.

Even before humans landed on it, astronomers suspected that the moon is totally barren and lifeless. Unlike Earth, it is virtually devoid of any atmosphere and any water; one scientist once told a meeting of lunar specialists that it is a million times drier than the Gobi Desert. Totally unprotected, its cratered surface bears countless unhealed scars from billions of years of bombardment by meteoroids ranging in size from dustlike specks to rocks larger than the island of Manhattan.

Because of the absence of clouds and weather, the moon experiences extreme changes of temperature. Under the sun's merciless glare, the moon's unshielded surface heats to more than 121 degrees Celsius (250 degrees Fahrenheit) during the two-week-long lunar day. But when the equally long lunar night comes, it cools to as low as −168 degrees Celsius (−270 degrees

Fahrenheit), which is far chillier than the lowest temperatures ever recorded in that terrestrial deepfreeze, Antarctica. To make matters worse for any would-be homesteaders in this hostile setting, the moon is assailed by dangerous cosmic rays and the sun's searing ultraviolet radiation; either could destroy life.

Still, we have already shown that humans can live on the moon, if only for brief intervals. During each of the six Apollo missions between the summer of 1969 and the winter of 1972–1973, twelve Americans spent up to three days on this forbidding surface. While much of mankind watched their televised antics with a mixture of awe and disbelief, the astronauts ventured three miles from their spindly, four-legged lunar module—at first on foot and later in electrically powered carts.

During their "EVAs" (space jargon for extravehicular activity), the lunar explorers crisscrossed small craters, descended into ravinelike lunar rilles, and panted up small hills. Moving with kangaroolike hops in the moon's one-sixth gravity, they looked more like schoolboys on a playful romp than like Earth's first envoys to another world. For all the lunar merriment, including such "unauthorized" capers as driving a golf ball before the TV camera, the men did their job extremely well; they set up many scientific instruments, including seismographs that are still radioing the occurrence of periodic moonquakes, caused by gravitational strains that build up when the moon moves closer to Earth or the sun. They also exposed thousands of frames of film, giving scientists invaluable views of the lunar surface, and amassed such a large collection of rocks and soil (381 kilograms or 841 pounds) that researchers have still not finished studying it.

Nonetheless, Project Apollo did not solve all lunar mysteries. On the contrary, the wealth of information raised new questions. For example, how did the moon get to where it is today? Some scientists contend that after the moon was formed, along with the sun and its entire family of planets, in the great rotating disk of gases and dust called the solar nebula, it strayed close to the young Earth and was captured by its gravity. But other researchers propose a different scenario. They say that the moon formed slightly later in the solar system's turbulent early years, out of a halo of rocks and debris, like Saturn's rings, circling the primordial Earth.

Despite the arguments, other important pieces of the lunar puzzle have fallen into place. From their careful analysis of the moon rocks, scientists are now agreed that the moon underwent a severe bombardment by asteroid-sized bodies, some scores of miles in diameter, in the first few hundred million years of its 4.6-billion-year history. These impacts gouged out huge craters; they also apparently created the great lava flows from the moon's interior that formed the lunar *maria* (pronounced *MAH-ree-uh*), or seas. Earth presumably experienced a similar assault, but the effects of the pounding have long since been erased by wind, rain, glaciers, and other geological erosional processes that do not occur on the moon.

Scientists also obtained precise information on the makeup of the moon's surface. Like Earth's crust, the moon rocks are rich in silicon, aluminum, iron, and oxygen; they also have a high concentration of the light space-age metal titanium. The moon is also extremely short on carbon, nitrogen, and, above all, hydrogen, the simplest of elements and part of water (H_2O). This absence was not unexpected; because hydrogen is so light, it apparently escaped the moon's gravity early in lunar history, although some scientists haven't given up hope of finding some lingering traces of it and possibly water as well. In fact, on the whole the moon seemed so rich in material that many scientists could not resist the obvious conclusion: that in the future, because of the abundance of energy in space, this lunar treasure might be mined and shipped to Earth. Even the lack of water did not seem to be an overwhelming handicap. The miners could simply release oxygen locked in lunar rocks and combine it with hydrogen imported from Earth to form vital water at their encampment on the moon.

Project Apollo, of course, made no use of these lunar resources. Every ounce of food, fuel, oxygen, and gear required for the astronauts' survival was brought from Earth. And whatever could not be easily carried back with them was left on the moon. The result seemed slightly scandalous to many people: a multimillion-dollar junkpile of cameras, radios, and even lunar rovers, still available for the picking to anyone who can retrieve them.

Not that space planners had any other choice. The available technology was still too primitive to haul back all this baggage. Indeed, NASA's engineers had their hands full making sure that the astronauts themselves got back. For instance, to keep them from being roasted alive, their visits were timed to avoid the lunar noon, when the sun is at its maximum height over the horizon. Also, when the astronauts went outside their spaceship, they had to don bulky pressure suits and backpacks, which provided them with all their needs: air, water, a cooling system, two-way radios for communications with each other and Earth, and even some food (in the form of candylike snacks tucked inside their helmets). Still, they had to be extremely cautious. Had they stayed "outdoors" for much longer than their maximum EVAs of seven or eight hours, vital supplies would have been exhausted and their lives in jeopardy.

If we hope to open permanent bases on the moon, space engineers will have to do much better. Certainly, those hardy souls who are sent to build and operate the bases will need more comforts if they are to remain on the moon for any length of time. The colonizers will also have to begin using the moon's own resources rather than extravagantly carting all supplies from Earth. And before anyone can even seriously begin planning lunar bases, it will be necessary to figure out cheaper ways of getting to the moon than by prohibitively expensive Saturn rockets.

Part of the solution to that transportation problem is already at hand: NASA's much acclaimed—and sometimes criticized—

space shuttle, which is slated to make its first test flights in the late 1970s. (In fact, the prototype vehicle, appropriately christened *Enterprise* after the spaceship in the *Star Trek* series, was rolled out by NASA in 1976.) Though many people have attacked the shuttle as another space extravagance, the indisputable fact is that such a vehicle is essential to realizing any future ambitions for manned space flight. Unlike the Saturn rockets, the shuttle will be used again and again, making as many as one hundred flights between the ground and Earth orbit. In contrast, the Apollo Saturns flew only once; of the 110-meter (363-foot) stack that roared off the pad for each moon mission, only a tiny command ship splashed down into the Pacific Ocean, and even these capsules were never sent aloft again. As a result of relying on such expensive rocketry, NASA's bill climbed to more than $1,000 for every pound of payload lifted into orbit. Once the shuttle begins its flights, the tab may drop to only a fraction of that figure.

Though the shuttle's orbiter craft looks like a bloated DC-9 passenger plane, it is actually a remarkable hybrid, a cross of rocket ship, glider, and conventional jet aircraft. Like the Apollo moonships, it will get a powerful rocket boost on takeoff, rising vertically off the pad on the back of a large, cylindrical propellant tank. The tank, which looks like a Saturn first stage, will have two smaller solid-propellant rockets strapped to its side.

Yet as the shuttle soars off into the Florida sky, the lift-off will only vaguely resemble those of the thundering Saturns. Besides making less noise, it will pick up speed much more slowly. Thus passengers will feel far less discomfort than did the Apollo astronauts (who were especially trained to withstand high g forces) and will include people who have not participated in the space program in the past, among them women.

At an altitude of 43 kilometers (27 miles) the shuttle will jettison its two small solid-fuel tanks, letting them parachute into the sea. There they will be picked up by special barges, then

The first orbiter vehicle of the space shuttle, dubbed *Enterprise,* is rolled out at ceremonies in Palmdale, California, on September 17, 1976. Its first flight into space is scheduled for the early 1980s. *(National Aeronautics and Space Administration)*

brought ashore for possible reconditioning and another launch. At about 185 kilometers (115 miles)—or what is known as low Earth orbit in space parlance—the shuttle will release the main tank. But the tank won't make it back to Earth in one piece. Tumbling through the upper atmosphere, it will break into small pieces. Like meteors, they will heat up, and most should be destroyed in a flaming death.

By then, the orbiter will be on its own, circling Earth at a speed of 27,000 kilometers (17,000 miles) per hour. After a burst of its own smaller maneuvering rockets, the orbiter will climb higher to a more stable orbit of 386 kilometers (240 miles). There it will be able to perform many useful duties—deploying or repairing small unmanned satellites, staging experiments with the help of an on-board space laboratory (provided by NASA's West European partners), and, in the years ahead, tackling even more ambitious tasks. Not the least of these will be helping to assemble the components of space stations, which will be transported piece by piece into orbit by the shuttle.

Having completed its immediate assignment, the orbiter will then swing around and fire its rockets again. With that maneuver, it will reduce its speed and begin spiraling downward to an altitude of about 120 kilometers (75 miles). As the atmosphere thickens, it will begin providing enough "lift" on the shuttle's stubby wings for the final descent. Gliding downward at high speed, it will aim for one of the two 16-kilometer (10-mile) runways that will await it at opposite ends of the country—one at Florida's Kennedy Space Center, the other at Vandenberg Air Force Base in California.

Landing will be tricky. Because the shuttle has no jet engines that allow it to circle over the landing site, it will have to put down safely on the first try. But if all goes well, the shuttle should be ready for another flight into space within only a few weeks or even days.

Creating the shuttle has tested all of NASA's considerable skills. During its plunges through the atmosphere, for example, the orbiter's skin will have to withstand temperatures much higher than those experienced by any other aircraft, including the supersonic Concorde. The ship will also have to survive the stresses of lift-off and of rocket speeds. But even with those special capabilities, the shuttle is not the ultimate answer for manned explorations of space. It will only haul passengers and cargo into Earth orbit. For more ambitious journeys, perhaps to the moon or even the planets, space planners are counting on another vehicle.

Called the space tug, this will perform a service that befits its name. It will be the workhorse of space, like trucks, freight cars, and tugboats on Earth. In early versions, which are already on the drawing boards in rough outline, the tug will be cylinder-shaped and will be carried aloft inside the shuttle's cargo bay. When the mother ship reaches low Earth orbit, this compartment will be opened up and the tug lifted out by a remote-controlled crane. After the shuttle has pulled away to a safe distance, the tug will fire its small rocket engine, which will boost it to a higher orbit or even free it entirely from Earth's gravitational grasp. Because such maneuvers are much easier in orbit, when the ship is already traveling at high speeds, the tug's engine can be much less powerful than the rockets of the space shuttle.

A space shuttle preparing to unload its cargo, possibly a component for an orbital space station, as it circles high above Earth. *(National Aeronautics and Space Administration)*

There will be plenty of work for the tug. Operating entirely automatically with no one on board, it could park satellites in what scientists call geosynchronous orbits, which are beyond the reach of the shuttle. These orbits are 37,000 kilometers (23,000 miles) high and are called geosynchronous because objects at that altitude move at the same speed as Earth's own rotation; thus they remain fixed over the same spot on the ground. Satellites in such orbits are extremely useful as relay stations for radio or television signals, as outposts for monitoring weather, and even as electronic navigational aids for planes and ships.

In the future, tugs could be used to release and service more complex satellites, including NASA's projected large space telescope—a 228.6-centimeter (90-inch) remote-controlled mirror that will produce exceptionally clear views of the universe from its perch above Earth's obscuring blanket of air. The telescope's images will be relayed to astronomers on the ground by television-type links.

Working in tandem with the shuttle, the tug will also help enlarge man's own activities in orbit. Encouraged by the success of the three Skylab missions, U.S. space officials—and presumably their Soviet counterparts as well—are already thinking about more ambitious programs: space stations so large and so well equipped that people will be able to live aboard them for a year or longer. How will such mammoth outposts be set up? The only practical way will be to launch the components piecemeal and assemble them in space, like parts of a giant Erector set.

That should be an ideal assignment for the shuttle and tug. First, the shuttle will carry the station's components, or modules, into low Earth orbit. Then they will be transferred to the tug, which will raise them into a higher orbit, where workers can begin putting them together. Why use two vehicles for a job that one should be able to do? Because the shuttle alone would have to carry so much fuel to get off the ground and reach high orbit that its payload of cargo would be quite small. On the other hand, by dividing the work between ships that have been designed to perform certain tasks with maximum efficiency—the shuttle for getting off the ground, the tug for working in space—the job becomes much easier and less expensive.

No exact designs exist yet for these second-generation space stations, but we already have some idea of what they will look like. Stacked like tuna-fish cans to form multilevel cylinders, the first stations will accommodate only from six to twelve occupants. The choice of personnel will be dictated in part by the station's assignments. Besides comfortable living quarters, each station will have laboratories, a workshop, a communications center, computers, dispensary, and a recreational area.

Later, as space knowhow increases, the stations will grow. More modules may be attached; the number of occupants will double or triple. Eventually, even the shape of the stations will change. Radiating out from a common center, the modules will form spokes and finally a wheel. Such a design has a special advantage. If the wheel is rotated at just the right speed, the centrifugal forces in the outer rim will simulate gravity for anyone living or working there. Yet if a weightless environment is needed—say, for casting extremely pure metals—scientists can perform the experiments in the station's central hub, where zero-g will prevail.

Many different types of activities could be undertaken in such a wheel in the sky. Besides zero-g experiments, scientists could set up an observatory that would keep watch on the sun, stars, and more distant objects in the universe. The station could also serve as a platform for viewing Earth. Military leaders have long sought such a perch to keep tabs on ominous moves by a potential aggressor. But it could also have purely peaceful duties. As NASA's unmanned Landsat satellites have shown, a bird's-eye view of Earth can lead to the discovery of hitherto-unknown mineral deposits, keep watch over forests and crops, and even provide early warning of droughts and of oil slicks and other pollutants.

Impressive as they may sound, such applications are only a small beginning. In the not too distant future, space stations may well become staging areas for lunar bases. In fact, even before Gerard O'Neill and others suggested the use of lunar material as building blocks for colonies at L5, other scientists argued for similar colonies on the moon. Some have even envisioned the construction of entire cities on the moon, perhaps encapsuled in great transparent domes or buried under ground to protect the moon people against their world's harsh environment. Earth's nearest neighbor could be, in Arthur Clarke's words, "the first stepping stone to the riches of the whole universe."

As it happens, the moon's own riches provide an enticing starting point. Besides offering a wealth of minerals, some of which are already becoming increasingly hard to mine on Earth, the lunar surface has other attractions. Paradoxically, one of these is a feature that will make life there difficult and dangerous. This is the moon's lack of air which would mean death in only minutes for any astronaut whose pressure suit failed—he would die from absence of oxygen and not, as some writers have suggested, from being torn apart. But such an atmosphereless environment can be extremely useful since it provides what engineers call an exceptionally "hard" vacuum. Not even the most efficient pumps on Earth can re-create comparable conditions, though engineers have never stopped trying to achieve them. The reason is that such vacuums would be ideal for certain manufacturing processes—for example, the fabrication of thin-film electronic components ("chips") for computers, pocket calculators, and other solid-state gadgetry: all these must be produced in ultra-clean environments.

Another lunar attraction for industry is the low gravity. Many precision processes, such as the casting of ball bearings or the creation of alloys, could be undertaken with somewhat better results in the absence of Earth's strong gravitational attraction, which interferes with the mixing of molten metals in foundries. Even healing might be helped in the lunar environment. Low-g hospitals established on the moon might speed the recovery of heart patients, for example, by easing the strain on their bodies created by normal gravity—though they might be subjected to brief stresses getting there.

The moon would especially appeal to astronomers. It would not only give them a better view because of the absence of an atmosphere but also let them cast larger mirrors in the low lunar gravity. In addition, since the moon rotates so slowly—only once a month, as it circles Earth—they could keep celestial objects under continuous surveillance for days at a time, whereas terrestrial observatories can work only a few consecutive hours. Radio astronomers would have a particular advantage. Antennas erected on the moon's far side—which never faces Earth—would be shielded from mankind's own increasingly louder radio noise. Such interference has been a major nuisance to astronomers in their efforts to pick up the faint beeps and squawks of such intriguing objects as quasars and pulsars.

Far-sighted space scientists not only are eager to establish the first lunar bases but also are giving thought to how they might do it. In their schemes, the space tug plays a key role. It will be used not only to ferry equipment and people to the moon but also to provide the first shelters there. Though these will resemble large cylindrical cans, they will be equipped with spidery legs and a propulsion system for landings and takeoffs.

As the tugs haul up more equipment from Earth, the base will become more complex. Different modules will be linked together, just as they were in Earth orbit to form large space stations. Some of these facilities may be partially buried under lunar soil as protection against the extremes of temperature and radiation. But the inhabitants will not be uncomfortable. Once the station has been completed, most of the work will be automated; computers will direct the mining and manufacturing facilities, with the station's personnel relegated largely to maintenance and supervisory roles. Sleeping quarters will resemble small staterooms aboard ships; meals will be served in cafeteria-style dining rooms. For recreation, the base may well have a library, a television room (where video cassettes will be available), and a gymnasium where personnel can keep in shape for the return to Earth and higher gravity.

Perhaps the closest counterpart of such a facility on Earth is the new U.S. base at the South Pole. Largely housed under a huge geodesic dome, which provides protection against the cold and the drifting snow, the station contains a complex of scientific equipment, including computers, as well as living and recreational facilities for forty people. The remote station in fact is completely self-sufficient. It operates for the six long months of Antarctic winter, when the entire continent is bathed in darkness and temperatures drop to −73 degrees Celsius (−100 degrees Fahrenheit) or less, in complete isolation from the rest of the world except for radio contacts.

The lunar base should perform at least as well and will be

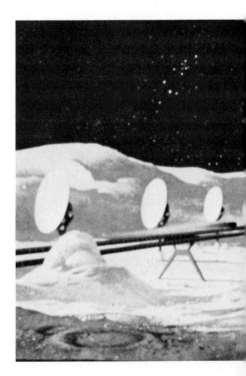

A mining base on the moon. In the foreground is a small transporter about to lift off. To the right are the camp's mining, living, and agricultural facilities. To the left is the magnetic track that fires buckets of lunar material off into space for use by the colony builders at L5. (From Science Year, The World Book Science Annual, Copyright 1975, Field Enterprises Educational Corporation)

extremely useful as a research and manufacturing facility. But should man's activities on the moon be expanded beyond that? Should Earthlings go to the moon simply to live there? Should it really be the site of large colonies? In the literature of space, many writers have strongly advocated lunar colonization, if only because the moon provides added living space for an ever-growing population. But others, with equal conviction, have argued against massive lunar colonization. Aside from its difficult environment, they point out, the moon presents a serious energy problem. Though sunshine is plentiful for fourteen days, these are immediately followed by fourteen more days when there is no light at all. For its survival, any lunar colony would have to store enough energy to last through that long night. Perhaps this could eventually be done with large batteries, or even with such energy-storage devices as spinning flywheels—the wheels would be rotated at high speed during the lunar day and their mechanical energy would be tapped during

the darkness to make electricity. Still, such technology would be extremely costly. To keep expenses down, planners probably would rely at first on conventional nuclear reactors. But these too are expensive. Also, they would export to the moon a problem that still has scientists baffled on Earth: How do you get rid of the dangerous nuclear wastes? Probably they would be buried, but that would require extreme caution by those involved in the work. The moon, to be sure, has one advantage as a site for nuclear power plants: if there was an accident in which radioactive material leaked out of the reactor, there would be no atmosphere to spread a deadly cloud of fallout across the lunar landscape.

Surprisingly, the moon's gravity is also a handicap. Though significantly less than Earth's, and thus highly useful for some purposes, it is nevertheless a force to be reckoned with. It must be overcome in order to leave the moon's surface. It cannot be shut off or reduced in strength, as can the centrifugal force of a space station. O'Neill has explained the situation in graphic terms. If humans traded Earth's gravity for the moon's, he says, they would be acting like an animal that struggles to climb out of a deep hole, only to let itself fall into a slightly shallower hole.

In his view, humans should try to avoid such gravitational holes when at all possible. Some bases on the moon will be necessary, he concedes, but they should have only a single purpose: to provide raw material for the construction of colonies in free space. Only a small contingent of people, perhaps no more than a hundred, will be needed to operate O'Neill's lunar base. Their job will be done largely by computers and automatic dirt-moving machines. But the really remarkable innovation in this scheme is what happens to the lunar material after it is excavated and packaged for export. It will not be transported to the colonies by space tugs or other kinds of conventional rockets but be fired off into space by a huge, futuristic version of an old-fashioned slingshot.

Controllers at work in the central station of the lunar mining base

6

Home at Lagrange

With almost evangelistic fervor, the proponents of space colonies have argued that the first people from Earth can be living in the bright-sunshine world of free space before the end of the century. But even these enthusiasts acknowledge certain practical realities. For one thing, there will have to be countless preliminary studies—testing materials, evolving colony designs, deciding what foods can best be grown in space, and, most important of all, finding out whether or not there still might be unsuspected biomedical perils for any humans who lived away from their home planet for long. Also, the space colony advocates will have to persuade political leaders that the idea—even if it is technically feasible—is really worthwhile.

Certainly, the effort involved in building the first colony will be enormous. The task might well take resources far greater than those of any single nation or even of several nations. Possibly the colony builders would have to form a worldwide consortium under the United Nations (if that body ever becomes truly united) or another international agency. But once the momentous decision to go ahead was made, there would be no shortage of scientific and engineering talent to turn the dream into a reality.

The short, brilliant history of the space age is in itself proof of our capabilities. Beginning with the Soviet Union's launching of the first Sputnik in 1957 and continuing through America's moon landing in 1969 and the more recent planetary probes as far out as Jupiter and Saturn, the leap into space has proceeded faster than even the most starry-eyed optimists could have hoped.

Exactly how would we turn these space skills to establishing the first colony? And, equally important, where would that pioneering venture be located? Already, there are plausible answers to these vital questions.

In a sense, one might argue that we have already tried our hand at setting up space colonies when we landed on the moon and sent Skylab into Earth orbit, if only for a very limited period of time. Both missions involved spaceships that were completely self-sufficient. If the Apollo astronauts had accidentally lost contact with controllers back on Earth, they would have survived at least until their food and fuel ran out. The Skylab teams were in a better position. They did not depend entirely on fuel from Earth; they drew most of their energy directly from the sun with the help of large electricity-generating solar panels.

With only a little more investment, Skylab could have been kept in operation for many more months, perhaps even years. Tapping sunlight, crew members could have started growing some of their own food aboard their space station. Admittedly the quantities would have been small; the orbital-grown crops could not have replaced food brought from Earth, but they would have stretched existing supplies. In addition, other measures could have been taken to lengthen Skylab's working life; oxygen could have been recycled and water extracted from wastes.

The key to success in such enterprises is not any new technology. Indeed, we already possess most of the necessary knowhow. It is the availability of cheap, abundant energy. In short, as long as the sun shines, there should be no trouble surviving in space.

The first full-fledged space colonies could be established high in orbit above Earth, but there would be some major drawbacks. As the colonies spun around the planet, they would frequently move into Earth's shadow; such eclipses would interfere, however briefly, with a colony's solar generators. Perhaps a more serious drawback of such a location would become apparent in the future. As satellite and space shuttle traffic increased near Earth, the number of colonies that could be safely placed in an Earth orbit would be severely limited.

Pondering these disadvantages of near space, scientists have long considered using one of the so-called Lagrangian points in the exploitation of space. Named after the eighteenth-century French-Italian mathematician-astronomer Joseph-Louis Lagrange, these points were "discovered" by him while he was trying to solve what mathematicians call the three-body problem. That problem can be posed in this way: if three celestial bodies—say, the moon, Earth, and an asteroid—are in orbit around one another, how will their gravitational and centrifugal forces act upon one another?

It was a difficult question and had long perplexed mathematicians, but the ingenious Lagrange found several solutions. One is especially significant. If the asteroid—or space station, if you like—were traveling in the same orbit around Earth as the moon, at a distance of 386,000 kilometers (240,000 miles) either ahead of or behind it, the smaller object, said Lagrange, would in effect be gravitationally trapped. It would always remain at the same distance from Earth and moon. The site ahead of the moon became known as L4 (meaning the fourth Lagrangian or libration point), the site behind it as L5. Lagrange's computations showed that there were three other points near the moon where bodies might be trapped for a while, but the forces there would not be stable and the object would eventually escape. (Remember: these sites or points are not really fixed but are moving with the moon, always keeping roughly the same distance from it.)

For many years, Lagrange's work was merely a footnote in the history of mathematics. But suddenly in 1906, an astronomical discovery rescued it from oblivion. Astronomers began

A diagram showing the relative positions of Earth, the moon, and the different Lagrangian points

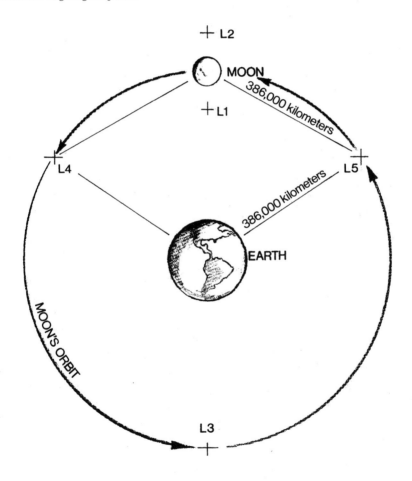

finding the first so-called Trojan asteroids, which were named after the heroes of the siege of ancient Troy, including Achilles. As the asteroids orbit the sun at the same distance as Jupiter, they cluster into two groups: one group travels ahead of the giant planet; the other trails it. Still more intriguing, astronomers found that the asteroids always maintain the same distance from Jupiter. The significance of these observations quickly became apparent. More than a century after his calculations, Lagrange's solution was vividly confirmed by observations of actual celestial objects. Just as he had predicted, any bodies located at L4 or L5 would remain there indefinitely. Note that the designations L4 and L5 can be applied to any three-body system.

Even before O'Neill suggested locating his first colonies at L5, other scientists had their eyes on the Lagrangian points. More than a decade ago, James Strong, a fellow of the British Interplanetary Society, which has long promoted the idea of colonizing space, suggested placing a communications satellite at one of the Lagrangian points in Earth's orbit of the sun. The purpose sounded very futuristic at the time: Strong wanted to provide some means of relaying radio signals to a spaceship or other human habitat while it was directly opposite Earth on the other side of the sun. In that position, the sun would block any direct-line radio signals to the distant outpost.

O'Neill and his young associates at Princeton were interested in the Lagrangian points closer to home. But when he began consulting other scientists about L5 in the Earth-moon system, he learned of an unexpected complication. Lagrange, he was told, had considered L5 only as a three-body problem. In fact, it is more complicated. To predict with accuracy the behavior of any large body, including a space colony, placed in orbit at L5, one would also have to take into account the sun's powerful gravity.

The solution to this four-body problem is even more difficult, but mathematicians, with the help of computers, have recently worked it out. The results indicate that when objects are placed at L5 (or L4), they will not remain rigidly in place. Instead, the sun's influence will cause them to move in a long elliptical orbit of up to many thousand miles around L5, like a ship swinging around its mooring with the changing tides.

Though this instability at first seemed like bad news to O'Neill's group, he and his students quickly realized that the wobble would not be a major handicap for space colonies. If anything is placed near L5, it will tend to circle the point. Even if the object is somehow disturbed, it will eventually drift back into orbit around L5. In fact, O'Neill argues, this gravitational eddy might be a decided advantage. Since they could be spread out, many colonies, perhaps even thousands, could be allowed to orbit L5, before the region became victim to a space-age version of urban sprawl.

Not that such overcrowding is an immediate danger. Even setting up a single colony at L5 will be a vast undertaking that requires a number of preliminary steps. Perhaps the most important of these is opening a sizable encampment on the moon. Its major purpose will be, not the manufacture of goods for Earth, but excavation of raw materials for the L5 colony. Why go to the trouble of mining the moon when raw materials could be sent directly from Earth? Because the necessary materials not only are plentiful on the moon but also could be lifted much more easily off the moon's surface; with the moon's weaker gravity, a rocket needs only 1/22 as much energy to escape from the moon as to escape from Earth.

The actual task of building the lunar base, as we have seen, is clearly well within our technological grasp. Even the transport of large amounts of heavy equipment to the moon would not be impossibly difficult. NASA planners have already envisioned a kind of space-age bucket brigade to do the job. The first stage of the voyage would have the equipment lifted by space shuttles to a rendezvous point in low Earth orbit. There the steady stream of shuttles would be met by waiting tugs; since these would be advanced versions of the original vehicles, they would have a larger payload capacity and could carry several shuttle-loads of gear.

When a tug finally fills up, it will fire its engines and head for the moon. Arriving three days later, it will be met in lunar orbit by still another type of transporter whose only task will be to ferry cargo from there to the moon's surface. Such a division of labor has special benefits. When each type of ship is given a particular duty in the bucket brigade to the moon, it can perform at maximum efficiency. This arrangement will not only speed up the transport but also keep down the bill.

In spite of the moon's harsh environment, mining there will be easy. It will require no special breakthroughs. In fact, the same earth-moving equipment used in the coal fields of Appalachia and elsewhere should work extremely well on the moon with only minor modifications. Since the moon's surface is not covered with any vegetation, these machines will simply scoop up the lunar soil—at rates as high as four tons a minute. Loaded onto conveyor belts, the material will be carried to another area where it will be compacted for shipment to the colony.

Such strip mining on Earth requires careful—and costly—restoration of the excavated area if it is not to begin looking like the moon. But since the moon is already battered and cratered, there should be no outcry over any environmental damage. In fact, even if the strip mining proceeded at a prodigious pace, it would be years before astronomers on Earth noticed the man-made crater even through their best telescopes. The building material for the entire first colony would require only the excavation of a pit about 4 meters (13 feet) deep, stretching over an area of about seven football fields. Still, it should be noted that the requirements for shielding might greatly increase these figures.

The job of transferring the lunar ore to the construction site in space will, however, demand ingenuity. Space tugs might

An overall schematic view of the traffic between Earth, the moon, and the colonies at L5. Note that the space tug, which carries passengers and cargo, departs from low Earth orbit rather than from Earth itself to conserve the enormous amounts of fuel needed for direct liftoff from the ground.

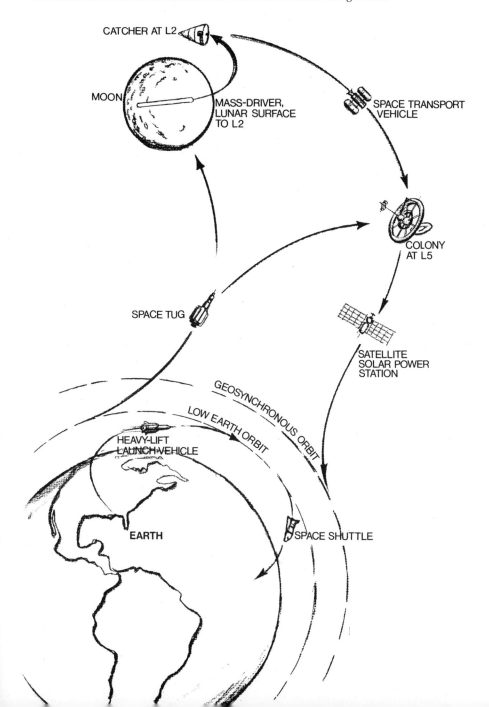

possibly be considered, but even with their enlarged capacity they will not be able to carry enough lunar ore for the colony's needs unless an enormous flotilla of such ships is built. Also, the exhausts of chemical rockets would create an atmosphere on the moon—and not a very pleasant one. To get around these problems, O'Neill wants to hurl the ore into space without any human assistance at all.

O'Neill says that this hurling could be done by a two-bladed rotary launcher. As the blades spun, they would release small pellets of compacted ore—perhaps weighing about five grams (1/5 ounce) apiece. The pellets would only have to reach a speed of about 2,400 meters (1 1/2 miles) per second to escape from the moon's grasp. If there were twenty-six such launchers, each driven by a 1,600-horsepower electric motor, O'Neill figures that half a million tons of lunar material could be transferred to the colony in six years. Except for some of the basic equipment that would have to be brought from Earth, this might be enough to construct a small, cylindrical colony for about 2,000 people, though possibly more ore would be required.

In any case, the scheme has another major shortcoming. Even if more material were hurled into space by setting up additional launchers, it would still have to be compressed into small pellets prior to launching. The compacting would not be especially difficult, but the small size of the pellets would make them hard to catch. Many might escape collection. And that too would slow down the delivery of essential ore to the colony.

Undaunted, O'Neill and his colleagues have proposed another catapulting system. It would rely on a so-called linear electric motor. As its name suggests, the motor is flattened out. Instead of spinning a rotor, it hurtles an object over a track. Already, such motors are being seriously studied by engineers as the basis for new transportation systems on Earth; since the moving part of the motor, which could be turned into a passenger car, is raised ever so slightly above the track by strong magnetic fields, there is virtually no friction. Only a small application of power could accelerate the car to high speeds. On the moon, the device would work even more efficiently since there is no air to slow it down or cause any instabilities in its movements.

O'Neill's lunar motor would be a spectacular sight. It consists of a closed loop about 10 kilometers (6.2 miles) long that looks somewhat like a large racetrack. Small buckets, each capable of carrying about 9 kilograms (about 20 pounds) of compacted lunar material, would be hurtled down the racetrack's guideway. Built into each bucket would be a set of powerful superconducting magnets; because they would be chilled by liquid helium to extremely low temperatures (only a few degrees above absolute zero), resistance to electrical currents virtually disappears, and the strong magnetic fields that are created would literally lift the buckets off the track. By the time the bucket reached the opposite end of the racetrack, it would easily have developed lunar escape velocity. Only a slight reduction of the bucket's speed would send its cargo flying off into space. Then the bucket would circle back to the other end of the magnetic raceway and pick up a new load, while another bucket moved its ore into launch position. In this way, as many as several buckets could be zipping up and down the tracks at any one time.

Of course, the launches will require extreme accuracy. But this should not be an insurmountable difficulty. As the buckets race down the track, their speed could be controlled with exceptional precision by beams of lasers; if a bucket's speed were only a tiny fraction of a second off, thereby endangering its aim, the laser would signal the error to a computer, which would automatically order the necessary speed up or slow down by adjusting the magnetic field.

Still another scheme for controlling the accuracy of the launches has been proposed by O'Neill and his colleagues. Each of the parcels of lunar material would carry a small electrical charge. As they lifted off the ground, the parcels could be slowed down, sped up, or otherwise deflected by an external electrical field that could be varied to correct errors. Exactly the same principle is used in present-day cathode-ray or television

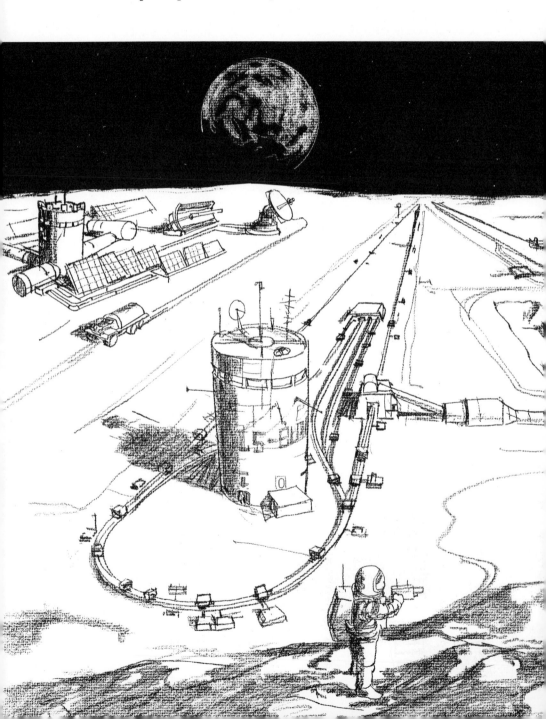

tubes; as the tube's beam of electrons speeds toward the screen, it passes by electrically charged plates that control the direction of the beam. The advantage of this system over the lasers is

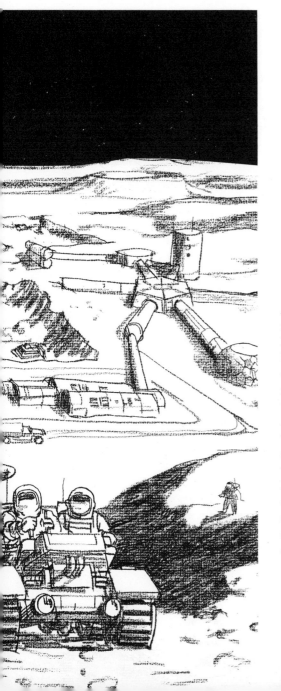

A typical "workday" at the lunar mining base. The loop-shaped layout of tracks is one of the base's magnetic launching devices for shipping lunar material into space for use by the colonists at L5. Like the Apollo astronauts, the workers would need to wear protective suits and carry their own oxygen when they ventured outdoors. But once back inside their climate-controlled pressurized quarters, this cumbersome apparel could be shed for ordinary clothing.

that it would probably be considerably simpler and cheaper.

The lunar-bucket brigade, in any case, could, in a single month, launch more than 50,000 tons of moon dirt, about the weight of a modest-sized cargo ship. At that rate, the construction crews in space could receive more than enough lunar raw material to complete the first colony within the allotted six-year schedule. But just to make sure that no crucial work time were lost because of equipment failures or maintenance delays, a second launcher would probably be built and kept ready for immediate standby use.

The basic mechanics of such an electromagnetic launching device on the moon were discussed more than a generation ago by author Arthur C. Clarke, who was then also an active communications scientist. So the principles are already quite well understood; moreover, recent work in superconductivity suggests that the scheme is not merely futuristic speculation. Still O'Neill acknowledges that the success of the launcher—which he calls simply a "mass driver"—is critical to the entire colony idea. Without such a relatively cheap system for getting the lunar building blocks into space, the colony would become hopelessly expensive and totally impractical. Nonetheless, on the basis of their preliminary studies, O'Neill and his colleagues are willing to take their chances with their proposed lunar mass driver. They are convinced that any engineering difficulties involved in its construction or operation could be solved well ahead of time in laboratories on Earth.

Transported in sections from Earth, the mass driver probably would be assembled on the moon's surface under a canopy of aluminum and lunar soil to protect the workers during its construction. A likely location might be relatively flat terrain in the moon's Descartes highlands. Explored by astronauts John Young and Charles Duke during the Apollo 16 mission in April 1972, this area appears to have a higher aluminum content than other regions of the moon; the samples brought back by Young and Duke consisted of up to 14.4 percent aluminum.

The mass driver would need considerable electricity. This could come from solar generators. But a likelier source is a nuclear power plant, which could keep producing electricity even during the two-week lunar night. Since the operation would depend largely on automation, only about a hundred and fifty people would be needed to run both the mining and the launching.

In his original proposal in *Physics Today*, O'Neill suggested aiming the compacted parcels of lunar material directly at L5. He explained that the journey would take only a few weeks, and by the time the payload arrived, it would be traveling about twice as fast as a pitched baseball, which would make it quite easy to catch. (If the ore were hurled at higher speeds, it would shoot out of the moon's orbit altogether.) But since that first paper, scientists have had second thoughts.

Lest flying debris from the moon score a stray hit on the colony, they have suggested keeping the barrage away from L5. They would aim the lunar ore instead at another Lagrangian point, called L2, which lies about 80,000 kilometers (50,000 miles) behind the moon's far side. Although anything placed there would not be as firmly anchored as objects at L5, it would be sufficiently stable to make a good target.

To snare the incoming barrage, space workers would set up a large metallic screen—or "catcher's mitt," as it has been dubbed—at L2. Again, the space tug would be the major workhorse. To keep the catcher's mitt from being knocked around by the impacts, it would have its own propulsion system to provide counterthrust. This could consist of a rotary catapult, like the original device envisioned by O'Neill for the moon, or some other type of mass driver, which would launch a spray of pellets manufactured at the site from some of the incoming lunar debris; only a small amount of material would be needed to do the job.

As the catcher's mitt filled, the moon stuff would be dumped into a large adjacent storage bin. Periodically, an ore carrier would arrive to take away the precious material. Like super-tankers on Earth, these space freighters would have enormous cargo capacity but would move very slowly. Also propelled by mass drivers, they would take as long as two months to make the journey from L2 to the colony at L5.

Everything in this operation, from positioning of the catcher's mitt to shipping the ore to L5, could be performed automatically by computers. A few maintenance people might be stationed in a small facility at L2, safely out of range of the incoming lunar material. They would act immediately if there were any breakdowns. Power for the catcher's mitt would probably come from a small nuclear reactor at first; later, solar energy systems might be developed that could meet the electrical requirements.

Once the ore carrier arrives at L5, it will begin unloading the lunar material at the colony's processing center. Kept at a distance from the principal living quarters, this large spherical working area will house solar-powered smelters to break the ore down into its components—aluminum for the colony's super-structure, silicon for its windows, oxygen for its atmosphere. Shaping the materials would be easier than on Earth; in the absence of gravity, huge aluminum sheets or beams, for example, could be extruded without any fears of breakage.

Some of the material will hardly have to be processed at all. Experiments with the Apollo moon samples have already shown that the addition of a little fertilizer turns lunar debris into a fertile soil in which plants flourish extremely well. Letting nothing go to waste, the colony's builders would even use the slag from their smelters. Pulverized into gritty sand, it would make an excellent material to thicken the colony's walls. That would help shield the inhabitants against cosmic-ray and other hazardous bombardments.

Before long, what first looked like a haphazard work camp would assume a recognizable shape as mankind's first permanent habitat in free space.

7

Building Island One

Exactly how the first colony—what O'Neill calls "Island One"—will be built can be described only in approximate terms. Certainly the ideas of O'Neill and other scientists will be radically altered and improved as their successors devise better methods of working in space. In fact, by the time construction is actually under way, scientists may look back upon the first groping designs with the same bemused interest we now show when examing the imaginative but crude ideas of such writers as Verne and Tsiolkovsky.

Still, we can engage in some reasonable speculation. Already several studies have shown that it will take no more than about 2,000 people—space-age hardhats—to do the work. To house themselves at L5, they will need a construction "shack" that will keep them in reasonable comfort for several years. They may even have small agricultural areas on which to grow some of their own food. One possible design for the shack is a sphere about 50 meters (164 feet) in diameter, sufficiently shielded to protect workers from overexposure to cosmic rays during the projected six-year construction period. Such a temporary habitat would have a number of public rooms (library, cinema, shops, lounges, and so forth), as well as about a thousand smaller living compartments, each with two bunks.

At the start most of the building materials for the construc-

A possible construction "shack" that could serve as a base during the building of a full-size space colony. Powered by its winglike solar panels and rotating around its central axis to create artificial gravity for the people inside, the shack is assembled piece by piece out of separate modules ferried into orbit by the space shuttle *(background)*. *(National Aeronautics and Space Administration)*

tion camp and Island One will have to be ferried from Earth. Entire sections of these initial facilities will have to be hauled piecemeal across a quarter of a million miles of space by relays of space tugs. In these early stages, food, tools, machinery, and virtually all essential gear will also have to be imported. But with each shipment, the construction team will become increasingly self-sufficient. Finally, when lunar ore begins to arrive, the future colonists will have taken a large step on the road to independence from Earth.

As construction proceeds at L5, one of the first tasks will probably be the assembling of aluminum work spheres about 100 meters (110 yards) in diameter. Pressurized with an earthlike atmosphere and heated to comfortable temperatures, these large metal balls—or "dry docks," as O'Neill calls them—will free the habitat's hardhats from the need to wear bulky space suits. Inside the spheres, workmen (and workwomen) will be able to put together additional sections of the colony in a shirt-sleeves environment. Even when handling bulky parts, they will not need cranes. In the zero-g environment of the spheres, these components could easily be moved by only a slight push with the hands. As each new section is finished, the workers will retreat to the safety of their living quarters. Then the aluminum sphere will be opened and the completed module pulled out by large remote-controlled arms like those used in nuclear power plants to extract radioactive fuel rods from reactors. Guided by controllers, the arms will position the newly finished component into the appropriate part of the budding colony. The sphere will then be closed and repressurized, and the workers will return to it for the assembly of the next module.

Meanwhile, a short distance away, other workers will begin putting together the catcher's mitt. Its huge netting and other components also will be ferried bit by bit from Earth. But the job will be much simpler and take less time than the work on the colony itself. Once completed, the entire structure will be towed to L2. That will be a milestone in the colony's early history: the

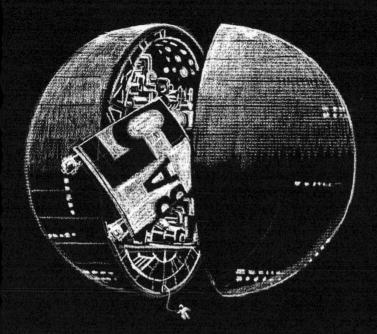

Two views of a construction "shack." After the fabrication of a component for the colony is completed, the shack can literally be split in half and the finished part towed to the colony site. Then the two halves of the shack are closed again, and work resumes inside on another part.

colony will begin getting its first raw materials from the moon. (Needless to say, even while the colonists are busily at work at L5, other hardhats will be completing the moon base and the mass driver.) Relying on sunlight to power their smelters and other processing machinery, the colonists will start fabricating major components for their habitat: cables and trusses for the colony's superstructure, aluminum and titanium sheets for its outer surface, metal-reinforced glass plates for portholes and solar mirrors. One by one, these parts will be bolted or welded together; the latter joining process seems to work especially well in the near-vacuum of space. Slowly, like a flower opening its petals, the overall shape of the colony will begin to emerge.

What that shape will be remains a matter of speculation. The joint study by Stanford University and NASA's Ames Research Center (see Chapter 2) considered various configurations, including cylinders, large spheres (appropriately dubbed "sunflowers" because they were surrounded by petal-like solar mirrors), a chain of smaller spheres linked together like a necklace, and even a stack of *2001*-type wheels, all spinning on a common axis. But after long deliberation, the participants in the symposium settled on a less radical design for the first colony. Their choice was a large tubular wheel with an overall diameter of 1.8 kilometers (1.12 miles) in which 10,000 people could work, raise families, and live almost suburban-type lives.

The study group picked the wheel for a number of reasons. It seemed relatively easy to construct, it would not have to be rotated more than once every sixty seconds to simulate Earth gravity, and it created a sense of spaciousness in its interior by offering a line of sight of more than half a mile. However, the price might seem high—the group figured that the wheel could be built for about $100 billion, about four times the cost of the Apollo program.

The Stanford torus, as the wheel was dubbed, closely resembles the space colony described by the imaginary new colonist in Chapter 1. The structure's total weight would be about 500,000 tons in Earth terms—roughly the tonnage of a large supertanker. The torus's interior would be bathed in sunlight reflected off an ingenious multiple-mirror system. This would consist of a large main mirror fixed at a forty-five-degree angle above the wheel, which would bounce rays of sunlight off a ring of smaller mirrors around the wheel's central hub. These in turn would reflect the light into the living area through louvres similar to Venetian blinds; the great benefit from the louvres would be to help keep out cosmic rays.

The strong sunlight would be extremely useful for growing a rich harvest of crops. It would also be tapped for generating electricity and powering the solar furnaces for refining the lunar ores. Most of these activities, however, will not be undertaken in the torus itself. They will be shifted to separate pods outside the wheel, where the colonists will be able to take advantage of the weightlessness and, for special metallurgical work, the high vacuum of space.

To most of the members of the 1975 Stanford–NASA study group—though not to O'Neill—the wheel seemed the best choice for a first effort. Their decision was based on both economic and engineering considerations. For one thing, since the wheel's surface is highly curved, and thus quite strong, its walls can be thinner than those of other configurations. Also, the volume of air needed to fill the cylinder is less than that required in other designs with comparable living area. But everyone agreed that, whatever the torus's attraction for an initial colony, other models might in the long haul prove equally suitable and perhaps even superior.

In fact, the ink was barely dry on the group's preliminary report before some scientists began issuing sharp dissents. After examining the design, one group at the Massachusetts Institute of Technology had no hesitation in pronouncing the Stanford torus structurally unsound. Their analysis showed that at the proposed atmospheric pressure inside the wheel (about 40 percent of that at sea level on Earth), small cracks and flaws

Sketches of the various designs under consideration for space colonies

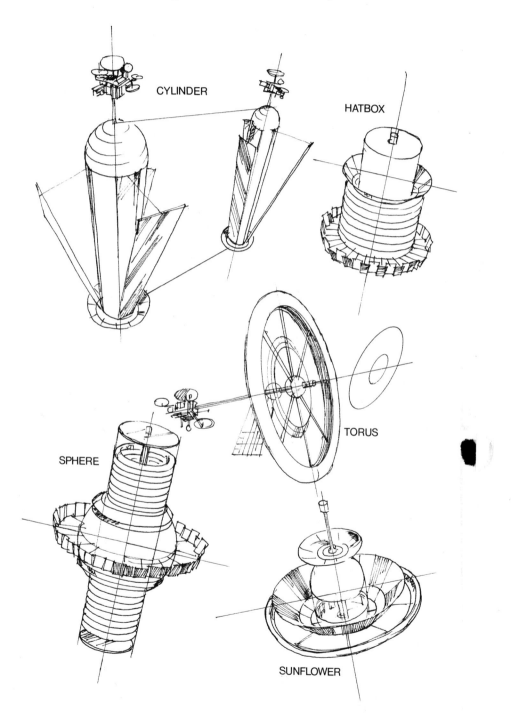

would develop in the torus's metal skin. Warned one of the critics: "The design would split like a dropped melon."

The defenders of the wheel disputed this analysis, arguing that far too little was known about the behavior of metals under such conditions to make any firm predictions. Nevertheless, they did concede that shielding around the wheel might have to be thickened to protect the inhabitants against cosmic rays, which seemed more threatening than anyone had originally anticipated.

Even while this sometimes emotional argument was going on, other designs began attracting interest. One was the so-called hat box, which was proposed as a first colony by a 1976 summer study at the Ames Research Center. Some 470 meters (500 yards) in diameter, it would have living space for about 6,000 people inside ten hollow rings stacked atop one another like a cluster of bracelets on a woman's wrist. Though the interior area of each ring would be relatively small, the inhabitants would not feel too cramped since they could travel from one level to the next, probably by escalators, as in a multilevel shopping arcade. They would also have a sense of space for another reason. The inner surface of the rings would be made of glass because they would not have to be shielded from cosmic rays. So, wherever one stood, one could easily look up at different levels of the colony. In fact, because of this shimmering, glassy look, the design quickly got another nickname—"Crystal Palace," after a famed glass-and-steel-girder exhibition hall erected in nineteenth-century London.

Another design unveiled by O'Neill while he was taking part in the same summer study group also looked to the past. It was an updated version of the Bernal sphere first proposed by the British physicist-futurist J. D. Bernal in the 1920s. A more advanced type of habitat that could be built during the first generation of space colonies, this hollowed-out miniworld is nearly a mile in circumference and has room for some 10,000 people to live on its inner surface.

While it might be somewhat more difficult to construct than earlier designs, the Bernal sphere is the choice of many scientists. It would have an overwhelming attraction: its large, unobstructed interior volume would give the colonists an almost earthlike sense of spaciousness. There would be none of the claustrophobia that might occur in the wheel. Even so, new colonists might find their first stroll in the sphere a little

Looking down from a hillside picnic *(lower right)* on the pleasant, countrylike interior of a Bernal sphere-type colony. Along the colony's central axis, a colonist amuses himself by flying a pedal-powered plane in that low-g region. Painting by R. Guidice. *(National Aeronautics and Space Administration)*

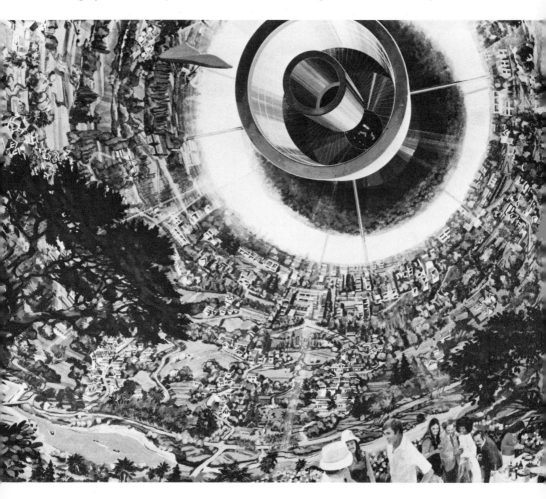

disconcerting. If they looked directly overhead while standing on the sphere's equator, they would see people, foliage, and buildings all apparently hanging upside down as though suspended from a ceiling; none of these would fall, of course, because the sphere's rotation (1.9 revolutions per minute) would create the same gravitational effect anywhere along the equator. But as they walked away from the equator, they would experience less and less gravitational tugging. Finally, when they reached the poles—the sphere's axis of rotation—they would feel completely weightless. For that reason, such low-gravity activities as human-powered flight might become a favorite polar recreation.

If nothing else, the variety of imaginative designs shows that the human bent for diversity probably will continue in space. Probably the cosmic architects of the future will not follow a single rigid pattern but instead design settlements of all sizes and shapes. While it is not necessarily the favorite, the configuration that has been most widely discussed is neither the sphere nor the wheel, but the cylinder. Indeed, that was the very first configuration to grow out of the original studies by O'Neill and his students at Princeton. Moreover, they suggested the construction, not of single cylinders, but of linked pairs.

In the initial O'Neill colony, each of the cylinders would be 1,000 meters (1,093 yards) long and 200 meters (219 yards) across. They would be positioned parallel to each other, like two side-by-side chimneys, and they would always point to the sun in order to catch its precious rays.

Like the Bernal sphere and the Stanford torus, the coupled cylinders would house a total of 10,000 people. Again, they would live on the inner surfaces, which would be divided lengthwise into six strips of equal size. Three of these would be land areas ("valleys") carpeted with lunar soil for living space, agriculture, and parks; the other three would be window areas ("solars") that would let in sunlight. The two types of strips would alternate like the black and white markings on a zebra.

In weightless environment, workers are easily able to maneuver large mirror panels into position during construction of a spherical space colony. Painting by Donald Davis. *(National Aeronautics and Space Administration)*

Like all the other colony designs, the cylinders would rotate, creating an artificial gravity to hold "down" people, animals, soil, buildings, and any other objects.

Overall view of several large cylindrical colonies as they would appear to an approaching spacecraft. The smaller modules ringing the main cylinder are agricultural stations. Hovering nearby are the colony's factories, where refining and other metal processing is taking place. (From Science Year, The World Book Science Annual, Copyright 1975, Field Enterprises Educational Corporation)

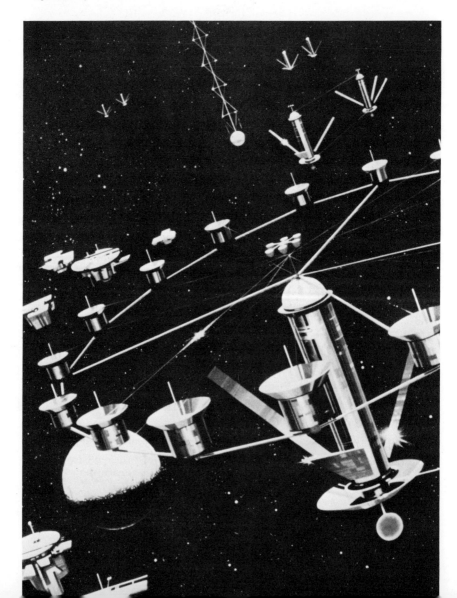

By pairing the cylinders, O'Neill neatly solves a problem in mechanics that will have to be dealt with by all habitat designers. As a colony spins, it behaves like a gyroscope (or a top), its axis of rotation always pointing in the same direction. Thus, as the colony makes its passage around the sun (along with the moon and Earth), the sun's rays will hit it at different angles. Though the change will be gradual, the result will be significant: the colony's mirrors, which are essential for reflecting the precious radiation into the living and growing areas, will gradually lose their fix on the solar disk. Somewhat the same thing would happen if a ground-based telescope aimed at a star did not have a tracking mechanism to compensate for Earth's rotation.

In some designs, the colonies will periodically realign their mirrors with small thruster rockets to keep the sun in sight. But as the colonies grow larger and the mirrors become more massive, much larger forces will be required for such maneuvering. In the O'Neill colonies the solution should be easy. The cylinders will be linked together—by a cable under tension at one end, and by a tower under compression at the other—and rotated in opposite directions. Thus the cylinders will cancel out their opposing gyroscopic tendencies, and it should be a simple matter to keep their mirrors precisely locked on the sun.

The life-giving rays would be captured at the far end of the cylinders—that is, the end away from the sun—by a large parabolic, or dish-shaped, mirror. Focused onto boiler tubes in the colony's power plant, the highly concentrated light would heat up gas, perhaps helium, and create enough pressure for the gas to drive a turbogenerator. Such a system could meet all the colony's electrical needs.

Sunlight for the cylinders' interior would come from three large, flat, rectangular aluminum mirrors. Hinged to the far end of the cylinder, they would reflect the sun's rays directly through the windows. The arrangement has a special feature: the mirrors can probably be swung open or closed to simulate a twenty-four-hour day-night cycle or any other arrangement the colonists prefer. All they would have to do is adjust the length of the cables attached to the free end of the mirrors, which keep them from flying off into space as the cylinder rotates.

As they looked up at the mirrors from inside the cylinder, the colonists would see the bright reflected image of the sun.

Looking from the endcap through a large cylindrical colony at the habitat's lush landscape. The sun, seen overhead through one of the colony's large mirrors, appears partly obscured by the moon during a solar eclipse. Painting by R. Guidice. (*National Aeronautics and Space Administration*)

Moreover, by slowly changing the angle of the mirrors during the twenty-four-hour cycle, they could make the sun seem to rise and set just as it does on Earth. Later, as they became more sophisticated in their technology, they might want to shorten or lengthen their day for the best growing conditions. Such manipulations could even create seasonal changes; these could be controlled in part by adjusting the height to which the sun rises in the colony's "skies." More intriguing still, the colonists could phase the seasons in the two cylinders so that it would be summer in one and winter in the other. If some of the colonists then decided they wanted a sunny holiday when their cylinder is experiencing winter, they could flee "south" to the other cylinder, where it would be summer.

Though the first crews of workers would have to bring along oxygen tanks from Earth, the completed cylinder would have its own atmosphere; the oxygen would be a by-product of the smelting of the lunar rocks. Combined with hydrogen shipped in from Earth, this oxygen would also be used to make the colony's water. As the years passed, the interior of the cylinders would become quite attractive. Large sections of the valleys would be devoted to grass, trees, ponds, and streams. Birds could also be released; the waterways would be stocked with fish. The colony's inhabitants would live, not in the valleys, but in small, bungalow-type homes in villages at either end of the cylinders.

Life could be very pleasant. Though 5,000 people would live in each cylinder, population density would be no worse than that in a block of old brownstone dwellings on a terrestrial island—Manhattan. Unlike Earth cities, however, the colonies will have no pollution. Fossil-fuel-burning vehicles would be banned. If the colonists wanted to get from one end of a cylinder to the other, they would walk or bicycle. Later colonies might install electrical tramways or moving platforms.

Most industrial or agricultural activities would take place, not in the cylinders, but in a halo of small spheres around their near (or sun) ends. Besides creating more living space within the cylinders, these pods have another purpose: their environments can be individually controlled to suit the activity inside them. For example, if you wanted to grow wheat in a pod, you would probably keep its climate drier and cooler than if you were cultivating fruit trees. To reach these work areas, the colonists would ride an elevator traveling through the spokes that link the halo to the main cylinder.

Perhaps the most novel feature of the colony would be the recreational opportunities. Since climate can be controlled, the colonists could pursue most outdoor sports, including skiing, sailing, and even O'Neill's personal favorite, soaring. But there would be a new wrinkle to these sports. Because the cylinder's artificial gravity diminishes as one gets closer to the center, O'Neill envisions some zany effects. If you tried climbing a hill, for instance, you would feel progressively lighter as you got higher; by the time you reached the top you might not weigh anything at all. Another amusement might be provided by a low-g swimming pool. The colonists might even try their hand at flying small, single-seat airplanes whose propellers are driven only by pedal power. Such man-powered flight is extremely difficult, if not impossible, in normal gravity. But as Arthur Clarke pointed out in *Rendezvous with Rama,* a sci-fi tale about a cylinder from a distant solar system, such a joy ride would be high adventure inside a space colony.

Indeed, after the initial construction work, the colonists would have plenty of time for such activities. By then much of the work would be mechanized. Food would become increasingly earthlike. All sorts of things could be grown, from staples like rice and potatoes to such exotic fruits as avocados, papayas, or mandarin oranges. Beer and wine would not be hard to brew if the colony decided to allow alcoholic beverages. (Based on terrestrial experience with Prohibition, the odds are it would permit liquor.) In addition to fishing in their streams, the colonists could meet their protein needs by raising chickens, turkeys, rabbits, and pigs. The only food that they might have to

Youngsters of the future trying their skills at low-gravity football inside a space colony

give up is beef since cattle probably would take too much space; a few dairy cows, however, would be kept for milk and cheesemaking. Giving up beef entirely might not be too much of a hardship; the craving could perhaps be satisfied by meat substitutes made from soybeans and other plant products.

There would be some dangers in the colony. The colonists would have to take strong precautions against fire since it could knock out machinery essential for survival. But enough safeguards, including duplication of key equipment, could be built into the system to reduce the risks. Meteoroids might also be an occasional hazard, but an extremely small one. Most meteoroids are microscopic in size and could not penetrate the colony's tough skin. If an occasional rock did crash through a window or wall, there still would be no real cause for alarm. It would take at least a day or so for the colony to lose its atmosphere, giving repair crews plenty of time to make a patch. But the chances of such a hit are very small—about once in ten million years. Moreover, scientists now believe that most meteoroids originate from the break-up of comets, which are composed largely of ice and dust particles, rather than from rocky asteroids. Consequently, getting hit by a moderate-sized meteoroid would probably be more like being struck with an easily pulverized snowball than with a hard rock.

Cosmic rays would represent a somewhat greater danger, but the colony's heavy shielding and atmosphere should provide adequate protection under normal conditions. If the flow of cosmic rays suddenly became more intensive—because of the eruption, say, of a solar flare—the colonists could retreat to special chambers with heavy walls until the menace passed.

The colonists might be subjected to more subtle physiological problems. The Skylab flights showed that the prolonged absence of gravity can affect muscles, change hormone balances, and weaken bones because of a loss of calcium. But since the colonists will experience zero-g for no more than a few hours at a time, during work in the pods perhaps, or even during play, it

Workmen making repairs in the colony's "skin." While meteoroid hits that could cause significant damage are highly unlikely, crews could be quickly mobilized to make a patch before the colony lost significant amounts of air. Here the workers are inside the colony and are wearing their oxygen-supplying pressure suits only as a precaution.

would present no special hazard. There is a chance, however, that the cylinder's artificial gravity might trouble some people.

If the colony's rotation is too rapid, it will intensify the so-called Coriolis force (which results from different sideways motions) and possibly disturb the body's sense of balance. The result might be a space version of seasickness, characterized by dizziness and nausea. The onset of such motion problems would vary with different people. There might also be more subtle long-term damage that might affect the ability of colonists to cope with Earth's gravity and environment, assuming they wanted to return occasionally or even to quit space altogether. To be on the safe side, the rate of rotation should be kept as low as possible. The spin in O'Neill's initial cylinders would be faster than some authorities recommend, but since the first colonists would be carefully screened for physical fitness, they probably would not be particularly bothered.

In any case, whatever hazards there might be would be offset by certain overwhelming advantages. Unlike Earth, the colony would not experience devastating earthquakes or volcanic eruptions or killing hurricanes and tornados, all of which have cost millions of human lives over the centuries. In addition, the colonists would not need to fear such nightmarish terrors as being bitten by a shark when they go swimming or attacked by a grizzly in the woods. Also, since the colony's population would be highly dedicated, like Israel's kibbutzniks or members of other communal groups, and would share fairly equally in a high living standard, there probably would be a minimum of violent crimes. Still, there might have to be a small lockup for the occasional transgressor.

By the time the first colonies are built, medicine will have made many more advances. But the battle against disease will still not have been won, and the colonies will require medical facilities, including small hospitals. In the event of a serious ailment beyond the capability of the local doctors—one requiring major surgery, say—the patient might well be sent to a neighboring colony that had a hospital specializing in that treatment. The trip by intercolony shuttle would probably be less jarring than that by an ambulance plane on Earth. One medical problem might demand special concern: because the colonists will be living in relatively close quarters, such communicable diseases as influenza would spread quickly. But presumably a society capable of building space colonies will have long since mastered the art of inoculating against such infectious ailments.

Besides growing their own food and perhaps producing special high-technology goods for Earth, the colonists would

Advanced colonies should have such spacious interiors that even structures as large as the San Francisco Bay Bridge will not dwarf the habitat. Whether the colonists decide to live in such bucolic settings or make their homes in space more citylike will be up to them. Painting by Donald Davis. *(National Aeronautics and Space Administration)*

have another job. Almost as soon as they finish their own cylinders, they will begin construction of offspring colonies. By this "bootstrap approach," O'Neill figures that each pair of colonies could be producing daughter cylinders at the rate of about two every six years. If, for instance, the first colony were completed by the 1990s, an admittedly optimistic target date, there could be dozens of additional habitats at L5 by the early part of the twenty-first century.

Yet replication will not be the colonies' only goal. Back in the 1960s, Dr. Peter E. Glaser, a space engineer in Cambridge, Massachusetts, suggested a novel solution to the energy shortage. He proposed placing a large solar-power satellite in geosynchronous orbit. Bathed in the sun's strong glare for nearly twenty-four hours a day, the satellite's solar panels—or turbogenerator, as Boeing engineers later suggested—could convert this energy into electricity, which would then be beamed down to receiving antennas on Earth in the form of microwaves. These in turn could be converted to ordinary electrical current, and the electricity could be fed into Earth's power grids.

Glaser pointed out that only a few large solar satellites could make a major contribution to Earth's energy needs. But his idea had an overwhelming drawback. The cost of rocketing the massive satellites into orbit would make the whole scheme prohibitively expensive.

Some people also fretted about possible environmental damage that might be caused by a beam of microwaves from space. For example, if any living things happened to stray into the beam's path for any length of time, they might well be "burned," just as they would be in a microwave oven. Yet such accidents would not be very likely. For one thing, the area where the microwaves are collected would be carefully cordoned off. Also, even if any people or animals did pass into the forbidden zone, the beam's intensity at any single spot would probably not be strong enough to do irreparable harm during only a single brief exposure.

For several years Glaser's solar satellites seemed no more than imaginative technological theorizing. But suddenly, amid all the talk about space colonies, a way appeared to turn Glaser's vision into reality. Why not build the satellites at L5? Using lunar ore, the colonists could not only fabricate products for themselves but begin to turn out satellite power stations. The technology would be no harder—indeed, it would probably be easier—than assembling a wheel or cylinder. Once such a satellite was completed, it could be towed to Earth by a space tug and parked in geosynchronous orbit to become the first extraterrestrial power plant.

The whole project sounds beguilingly attractive. It would take far less lifting power to bring the satellite from L5 than to rocket it off the ground. In addition, since the satellite's various parts would not have to withstand the jolting vibrations of a blast-off from Earth and would never be subjected to terrestrial gravity, they could be extremely lightweight. The satellite itself could be huge, perhaps several miles long.

For O'Neill, the advantages seemed overwhelming. His calculations indicated that if the colonists at L5 really set their minds to the task, their construction of satellite power stations could begin satisfying the United States's annual needs for new electrical generating capacity within only thirteen years. The total power beamed down from space would exceed that produced from the entire oil flow through the Alaska pipeline in only a few years. Even if the price charged for the electricity produced from satellites were no higher than today's typical electrical rates, according to the estimates of O'Neill and his colleagues, the income from the orbital power stations could be enough to pay for the entire colonization program—the lunar base, the L2 catcher's mitt, and the cylinders themselves—in barely twenty-five years. After that, even if the total bill for the entire L5 project totaled nearly $200 billion (O'Neill's highest estimate), the solar-power satellites would begin returning a handsome profit.

8

To the Asteroids and Beyond

As the space folk became more adept at living in their new world, they would become less and less dependent on Earth. Many of them might not even bother to return to their home planet for visits. For younger people born in space, Earth might only be a place that they had heard about from their parents or read about in the colony's library or seen on a video screen. Though it would shine even more brightly in their night sky than the moon (which would also be visible), it might eventually be regarded as just another planet.

With their increase in skills, the colonists would also become more ambitious. Instead of building carbon copies of their own miniworld, they would begin work on more complex homes in space. Such second- and third-generation colonies might well be cylinders but probably would include many geometries—wheels, spheres, hat boxes, sunflowers, to name only a few possibilities. In fact, as architects experimented with different designs, L5 might start to resemble a great metropolis whose skyline was silhouetted with towers of every shape and height.

Along with the increase in numbers, the colonies would grow in size and population. O'Neill's blueprint for the first colony—his Island One—calls for a habitat that would accommodate about 10,000 people. He originally conceived of it as consisting of two parallel cylinders, about fifty miles apart, but he concedes that it might be easier to start off with a sphere about a quarter of a mile in diameter. One argument in favor of the sphere is that it provides the greatest volume of air for a given surface area.

Whatever the shape of Island One, if construction proceeds on schedule, after about eight years there will be from eight to sixteen such communities at L5. That means that as many as 160,000 people could then be living in space. By that time, both population and construction skills will be sufficient to tackle the larger type of habitat that O'Neill dubs Island Two.

If space designers opted for more spheres, Island Two probably would be a giant globe a little more than 1,800 meters, (1 mile) in diameter and 6.4 kilometers (4 miles) in circumference, housing some 140,000 people. Island Two could also take the shape of two parallel cylinders. To accommodate that large a population, each cylinder would have to be some 3.2 kilometers (2 miles) long and about 640 meters (1/3 mile) in diameter.

Finally, after several decades in space, the colonists might begin work on a still more mammoth project. In O'Neill's view, since simplicity of construction would no longer be so important, Island Three probably will consist of cylinders (in which earthlike conditions can be more readily simulated). Each section of a two-cylinder habitat would be some 32 kilometers

(20 miles) long and some 6.4 kilometers (4 miles) in diameter. The interiors of these Island Three cylinders would be so huge that they would allow for an almost earthlike atmosphere, with clouds, rain, or other kinds of precipitation and even a blue sky. A pair of such slowly rotating cylinders could be the home for up to ten million people.

In spite of their larger size, O'Neill hopes to keep these later

Part of a torus-shaped colony as it would appear in the final phases of construction. The Venetian-blindlike louvres on the wheel's exterior would absorb dangerous cosmic radiation while at the same time allowing vital sunlight to be reflected into the colony's living and agricultural areas. *(National Aeronautics and Space Administration)*

The awesome view from one end of an advanced cylinder-shaped colony about 20 miles (32 kilometers) in length that could provide a home for millions of people. Because of the cylinder's rotation, even the clouds follow a circular path in the colony's "sky." Painting by Donald Davis. *(National Aeronautics and Space Administration)*

colonies from overwhelming their occupants. The interior of some cylinders might be modeled after a South Sea island; their climate would be balmy and their valleys filled with a colorful assortment of foliage. Other colonies might resemble small resort towns like Carmel, California, with small houses, shops, and tree-lined streets.

Above all, O'Neill hopes the colonists will not repeat the mistakes of city planners back on Earth. In a note to an illustrator instructing him on how to show the colonies, he wrote: "The whole idea is not to be monumental; keep the scale small and human. Please show the shops as highly varied: boutiques, bookshops, tiny restaurants, etc."

Only natural features would be allowed to reach terrestrial proportions. In the larger colonies, there could, for instance, be a mountain several thousand feet high; it would be made largely of moon dust atop a framework of steel and aluminum girders. Listen to O'Neill's rhapsodic description of this alpine setting at L5: "The upper part of the mountain is wild, just trees and rocks for climbing. There is a town on the lower slopes, rather like a version of San Francisco or a larger version of the Italian coastal town of Amalfi. . . . Cable-car tracks wind up the lower slopes of the hills. At the foot of the mountain, just in the valley floor, there is a lake with boats, marinas, beaches. . . ."

The colonies will also have other earthlike features. As their volume increases, they will begin to develop their own weather. Water vapor will accumulate in the atmosphere; clouds will form. Occasionally there will be showers—or perhaps snowfalls, if the colonists insist on them. But the rain or snowflakes will fall with a peculiar twist. Since the clouds will hover near the center of the cylinder, the precipitation will scatter in all directions, like the spray from a garden sprinkler.

The strange rainfall will not be the only bizarre effect. Because of the cylindrical colony's rotation, streams and rivers will appear to run uphill. As colonists look across the cylinder, houses will seem to be hanging upside down from the opposite surface. Even more disconcerting, if they happen to peek outside, the stars will appear to be spinning as the cylinder rotates. (If the colonists wanted to have an astronomical observatory, they would probably locate it in one of the pods of the nonrotating halo or in one of the cylinder's endcaps; from either platform, the stars would appear to be fixed.)

If life in space follows Earth patterns, different colonies will probably develop in their own unique ways. One colony might, for instance, opt for a Mediterranean-type culture with a warm

Workers in pressure suits building a mountain in zero-g environment

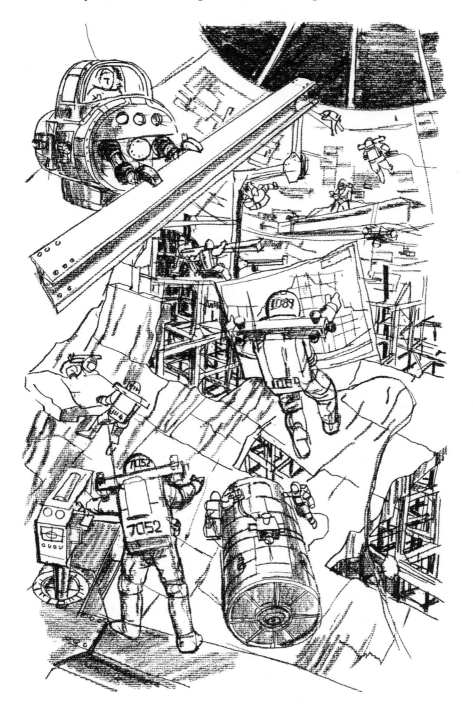

climate, spicy cuisine, many "outdoor" festivities, and a generally easy life style; another might pick a more conservative northern European pattern. Since the colonies will be about 120 miles apart for safety reasons, to avoid collisions, the distances are small enough to permit a little cylinder-hopping during vacations.

The shortest trip will be to the twin cylinder right next door. It will be a simple jaunt: you merely board a pilotless craft attached to the outer surface of your own cylinder. At just the right moment, it will unlock and be hurled into space by the cylinder's spin. Within a few minutes, the little space ferry will attach itself to the adjoining cylinder and disgorge its passengers through an airlock. Longer journeys, to colonies several hundred miles away, will probably use rocket-powered ferries under precise computer control. If you think such automation is beyond current capabilities, remember that both the United States and the Soviet Union have sent robot spacecraft across millions of miles with unerring accuracy.

Of course, if you really wanted a rest from space, you could board a shuttle for Earth. The flight will take about five days. On your return, you might make a stopover at the moon to examine the mining activities there. At first, such trips may have to be booked long in advance. But as the number of colonies grows and transportation facilities improve, they will be no more difficult to arrange than present-day jet flights to Europe or the Orient. Bookings would be made with a computer-controlled reservation system. At the appointed hour, you would appear at the space colony's docking tower, located in the cylinder's "nose," or sun end, and board the waiting shuttle. You could be fairly sure of on-time departures since space travel would not be plagued by the fickleness of terrestrial weather.

The first colonies will be populated by people especially picked for their skills and dedication. Also, because of their dependence on their home planet for many different materials, the early colonists will retain strong links with Earth. Workers

Ejected from the surface of a spinning cylinder, a small tube-shaped passenger vehicle carries colonists on a visit to a neighboring colony. Earth, a space tug, and another colony are in the distance.

will shuttle back and forth between Earth and L5 in regular rotation, like today's engineers and construction workers who take assignments abroad for a year or so. The leaders of the colonies will probably be able to make some decisions for themselves, but major actions will still need Earth's approval.

But as the number of colonies increases, small but extremely significant changes will take place. Some people might decide to spend their entire lives in space. Babies would be born, and old people would die; bodies would not be buried but be treated like any other organic material—something to be processed in the colony's recycling center for return to the ecosystem. Eventually the colonies might begin experiments at self-government.

In some colonies, final power might reside in an old-fashioned town meeting of the New England type, with all adults participating. Other colonies might be organized along corporate lines, with a president or general manager responsible to a board of directors, who would perhaps be elected on a rotating basis from the community at large. Underneath this top governing structure will be lower-ranking officials, each charged with specific duties. However the colonies are organized, though, the final say will reside with the colony's voting "citizens." In space, if not on Earth, democracy may yet become the predominant form of government.

Though they would have considerable independence, the colonies probably will find it desirable to form some alliances. These might simply take the form of loose trade groupings like the Common Market; presumably, since different colonies might specialize in the production of different manufactured or agricultural products, they would find it in their interest to barter with one another. These associations might also lead to closer ties, perhaps to a federation of colonies. One might even envision a United States of Space, formed after the colonies at L5 declare their independence of Earth.

Since human nature is the product of a long period of

evolution, only the most confirmed optimist would hope that it will show any overnight changes in space. Such ingrained emotions as love, fear, hate, passion, and so forth will continue to exist. People will still quest for power and pleasure; they will also need friendship, intellectual stimulation, and physical challenge if they are to survive as fully satisfied human beings.

Yet not all human shortcomings may be exported to L5, not because of the idealistic character of the colonies but because of the very nature of space itself—its almost unlimited resources of energy and building material. No longer will there be a need to scramble for land, bicker over the wealth of the seas, or contend for rich oil or coal fields. These resources, all essential to the growth of human society on Earth, will simply not be needed by the colonies.

Still, given the human race's long history of conflict, one can easily imagine continued mischief-making in space. A particularly ambitious colony, perhaps allied with a few like-minded colonies, might try to subjugate more peaceful colonies. Indeed, no one but a Utopian dreamer would say that there is no chance of war's breaking out in space. Yet, it could be asked, why will anyone want to fight? If imperialistic adventures produced no profit in land or resources for the conquerors, why would anyone embark on such adventures? Except as sheer displays of madness, such forms of aggression would become meaningless—and perhaps obsolete.

Earth, too, would undergo changes. As the number of colonies grew into the hundreds and even thousands, an increasingly larger proportion of the human race would live in space. After several centuries, Earth's population might be only a fraction of its size today. With fewer people to despoil them, the land, air, and seas would gradually recover from centuries of exploitation. The skies would become clear again. Forests would flourish. Rivers and lakes would cleanse themselves of pollutants. Even more heartening, such endangered animal species as the majestic bald eagle, giant blue whale, and almost-human orangutan might yet survive. Earth would finally become, in O'Neill's words, "a worldwide park, free of industry, slowly recovering by natural means from the near deathblow it received from the Industrial Revolution. A beautiful place to visit for a vacation."

Yet by that time Earth might only be a faint memory for most colonists. And as their need for raw materials increased, they will surely begin casting eyes on more distant targets—the asteroids. Most of these bodies circle the sun in a great belt between the orbits of Mars and Jupiter, perhaps the debris of a planet that failed to form or possibly exploded. Ranging in size from pealike grains to rocks several hundred miles across, the asteroids are a rich source of material. Some apparently contain iron and nickel, which could be easily turned into high-grade steel. Still others are rich in aluminum, silicon, hydrocarbons, nitrogen, and even water ice. If the colonists could tap these resources, they would virtually end any lingering dependence on Earth. Even precious hydrogen to make water would no longer have to be imported. In fact, the total material in the asteroid belt would supply the building blocks for enough colonies to create a living area 3,000 times that of the surface of Earth.

No great ingenuity would be needed to get at this untouched treasure. The job would be even simpler than mining the moon. All the colonists would have to do is send large freighters to the asteroid belt. The ships might even be pilotless; computers could direct them with sufficient navigational accuracy to catch up with one of the orbiting rocks. Indeed, an entire asteroid might be brought back to L5. Only a small amount of energy would have to be expended for such a round trip. For their propulsion systems, the ships would not rely on expensive chemical rockets but resort to the same mass drivers used by the mass catchers at L2. Moreover, the particles expelled by these devices could come from chunks of the asteroid cargo.

A large space vehicle from L5 attaches itself to an asteroid to begin mining its mineral resources for transport back to the mother colonies. Painting by Chesley Bonestell. *(National Aeronautics and Space Administration)*

As their ties with Earth loosened further, the space colonists might consider leaving for even more remote regions of the solar system. Some adventurous souls would settle near the asteroid belt. At first, these bases might simply be mining and manufacturing centers. But, later, some colonists might want to spend their lives there; as orbital homes go, the site might even be more

To the Asteroids and Beyond   129

desirable than L5. Still other emigrants might set up colonies near a planet—perhaps Mars, long an object of fascination to Earthlings. Before many more centuries elapsed, colonies would be scattered through much of the solar system.

The problems created by such moves should not be overwhelming. Since high thrusts are not needed to leave L5, entire colonies could break away under their own propulsion systems. As the colonies edged farther and farther from the sun, the amount of solar radiation would diminish, but the colonists could make up the energy deficit by using concentrating mirrors to "magnify" the available sunlight. Eventually, even such moves as these will seem unsatisfactory to some restless spirits.

Driven by the same inquisitive urges that have motivated all explorers from the first Asians who crossed into the New World during the last Ice Age to the pioneers who opened up the American West, these space folk will look beyond the solar system. And as the mastery of space increases, they will finally

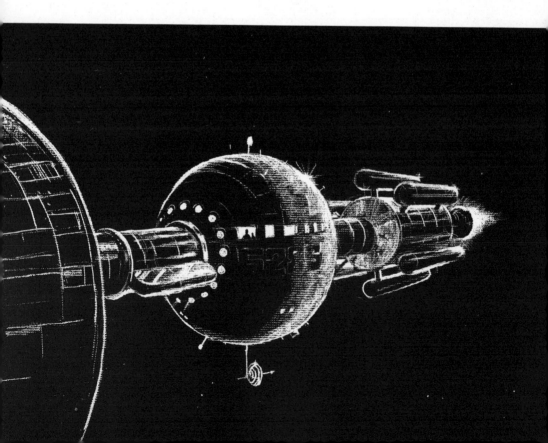

be able to yield to their impulses. By the twenty-second or twenty-third century, perhaps sooner, a cylinder, wheel, or sphere may begin the first journey to a nearby star.

Such an epic voyage might take many hundreds or even thousands of years unless the voyagers could somehow approach or break the universe's absolute speed limit: the velocity of light. But the travelers would be well prepared. Inside their star ship, life would continue as usual. Food would be grown. Industry would not cease. New generations would be born and earlier ones would die. Nothing would deter the ship's progress into the dim, cold reaches of distant space.

As the sun dwindled into a mere speck, just another star among the Milky Way's billions of stars, Earth itself would become only a dim ancestral recollection. But that will not matter. Those aboard the lonely ship will no longer consider themselves inhabitants of a single planet or solar system. They will truly have become star folk.

Glossary

Acceleration. The rate of change in the velocity or speed of a moving body, such as a spaceship.

Air resistance. The force that tends to slow down an object moving through the atmosphere.

Artificial satellite. A man-made object placed in orbit around Earth or another member of the solar system.

Asteroid. One of thousands of small bodies circling the sun chiefly between the orbits of the planets Mars and Jupiter.

Astrology. A pseudo-science based on the ancient view that heavenly bodies directly influence our individual lives.

Astronomy. The study of the heavens by observation and theory.

Atmosphere. The envelope of gases surrounding a planet or a star.

Atom. The smallest unit of an element—for example, an atom of hydrogen or carbon.

Comet. A relatively small collection of matter, consisting of dust and frozen gases, which travels through the solar system in a highly elongated orbit and "grows" a bright tail when it approaches the sun.

Computer. An electronic "brain" that can perform high-speed calculations and has special usefulness in determining the trajectories of spacecraft.

Cosmic rays. High-speed atomic particles, mostly protons, that travel through space. They could be a threat to space travelers.

Countdown. The time schedule, first in hours and later in minutes and seconds, for preparing a missile or spacecraft for launch.

Earth. The third planet from the sun and our home in space.

Eclipse. The sudden darkening of a heavenly body that occurs when another passes between it and the observer.

Electromagnetic radiation. The radiation produced by fluctuations of electric or magnetic fields in space. Visible light is an example of such radiation.

Escape velocity. The minimum speed at which a spaceship or other object can escape from the surface of a planet or other massive body.

g. A symbol for the gravitational force at Earth's surface. Thus 2g's are equal to twice that force.

Galaxy. A vast collection of stars held together by their mutual gravity. The Milky Way, which has some 250 billion stars, is one example.

Gravity (or gravitation). The basic force of attraction that exists among all matter in the universe.

Gravity, artificial. The outward pulling (centrifugal force) created by rotating a space station or other space vehicle to imitate the effect of true gravity.

Infrared radiation. Light detectable only by special instruments, which has a wavelength slightly longer than that of visible light. It falls into the range of radiant heat.

Jupiter. The fifth planet from the sun and also the largest in the solar system.

Lagrangian points. Points in space at which the gravitation and centrifugal forces of two celestial bodies cancel each other out, so that a third object placed at these points will tend to remain there indefinitely. Also known as libration point.

Light-year. The distance traveled by light, moving at a speed of 300,000 kilometers (186,000 miles) per second, in one year—roughly 9 trillion kilometers (6 trillion miles).

Mars. The fourth planet from the sun. Because of its rough similarity to Earth in size, tilt, and distance from the sun, it has long been suspected of harboring some life.

Mercury. The innermost of the sun's nine major planets.

Meteoroid. A small chunk of matter in space. When it enters Earth's atmosphere and starts to burn, it becomes a meteor ("shooting star"). If any fragment survives this flaming descent and reaches the ground, it becomes a meteorite.

Molecule. Two or more atoms linked together.

Moon. Earth's companion in space. Though other planets also have moons, our satellite is so large in comparison to Earth that astronomers sometimes regard the two bodies as a double planet system.

Neptune. The eighth planet from the sun.

Nuclear power. The energy released by splitting the nuclei of atoms (fission) or by joining them together (fusion). The latter, also known as thermonuclear power, is the process at work in the interior of the sun and other stars.

Orbit. The path of an object in space around the center of the gravitational system to which it belongs.

Payload. A missile's or spaceship's useful cargo, including instruments and passengers.

Planet. A satellite of a star.

Pluto. The ninth and outermost known planet of the solar system.

Re-entry. The return of a space vehicle or missile into Earth's atmosphere, which occurs at high speed and is accompanied by great heating.

Rocket. Essentially a chamber, from one end of which gases or other particles are expelled at great speed, thereby driving the chamber in the opposite direction by the recoil.

Satellite. A smaller body orbiting a larger one in space.

Saturn. The sixth planet from the sun, second only to Jupiter in size. Its rings make it one of the most spectacular sights in the sky.

Solar system. The sun and its entire family of satellites.

Space shuttle. A re-usable vehicle that can ferry passengers and cargo between Earth and orbit.

Space station. A more or less permanent orbital base.

Star. A celestial body that shines by its own light, which is produced by thermonuclear reactions, as opposed to planets, which are luminous only by reflected sunlight.

Sun. Earth's parent star.

Thermonuclear power. See Nuclear power.

Trajectory. The path followed by a missile or rocket.

Ultraviolet radiation. Light of a wavelength slightly shorter than that of ordinary visible light.

Universe. All of space, matter, energy, and time.

Velocity. The speed of a body in a particular direction. The term is often used to mean simply speed.

Venus. The second planet from the sun, ordinarily Earth's nearest planetary neighbor.

Weightlessness. The condition that occurs when a structure like a spacecraft and the people in it are accelerating together so that the passengers experience no resistance from the ship and are in a so-called free fall. Zero-g is often used as a synonym, although, to be precise, gravity never really vanishes.

Zero-gravity (zero-g). See Weightlessness.

Selected Bibliography

Books

Berry, Adrian. *The Next Ten Thousand Years*. New York: Saturday
Review Press/E. P. Dutton & Co., Inc., 1974.
Provocative look into the future by an experienced British science
writer.
Clarke, Arthur C. *Man and Space*. New York: Time-Life Books, 1969.
Lushly illustrated, well-written history of the space age up to the
Apollo program, by the well-known writer and scientist.
——. *Profiles of the Future*. Rev. ed. New York: Harper & Row, 1973.
A collection of essays about technology, space, and human
progress.
——. *Rendezvous with Rama*. New York: Harcourt Brace Jovanovich,
1973.
Fictional account of an invasion of the solar system by a giant
cylinder remarkably like O'Neill's, sent by a distant extraterrestrial
civilization.
Cooper, Henry S. F., Jr. *A House in Space*. New York: Holt, Rinehart &
Winston, 1976.
A veteran space reporter's absorbing account of Skylab.

Gilfillan, Edward S., Jr. *Migration to the Stars.* Washington, D.C.: Robert B. Luce Co., Inc., 1975.

A discussion of the possibilities for humans in space, including a fascinating scenario for colonizing a planet in another solar system.

Ley, Willy. *Rockets, Missiles, and Men in Space.* Rev. ed. New York: The Viking Press, Inc., 1968.

An almost encyclopedic history of the space age and its origins.

McCall, Robert, and Asimov, Isaac. *Our World in Space.* Greenwich, Conn.: New York Graphic Society, Ltd., 1974.

A noted space artist and a prolific author combine talents to provide a stunning portrait of the future in space.

O'Neill, Gerard K. *The High Frontier.* New York: William Morrow and Company, Inc., 1977.

The definitive book about space colonization by its most eloquent advocate; essential reading for anyone truly interested in exploring the possibility.

Ruzic, Neil P. *Where the Winds Sleep.* New York: Doubleday & Company, Inc., 1970.

An account of what it would be like to colonize the moon.

Taylor, L. B., Jr. *For All Mankind.* New York: E. P. Dutton & Co., Inc., 1974.

The story of the U.S. space program in the 1970s and beyond.

Tsiolkovsky, Konstantin. *Beyond the Planet Earth.* Translated by Kenneth Syers. New York: Pergamon Press, 1960.

An American edition of the turn-of-the-century prophecies about space colonization by the pioneering Russian space theorist.

Other Publications

L5 News. Newsletter of the L5 Society, 1620 North Park Avenue, Tucson, Arizona 85719.

Provides up-to-date reporting on the effort to awaken public interest in space colonization.

NASA Ames/Stanford University 1975 Summer Study, titled "Settlements in Space: A Design Study" (NASA-SP 413), editors R. D. Johnson and C. H. Holbrow. Published by Ames Research Center, Moffett Field, California 94035.

A good nontechnical description of the wheel design for a colony, as well as a solid overview of the problems and benefits of space colonization.

Newsletter on Space Studies at Princeton.
A periodic listing of the latest publications on the subject and other information.
Issued by Gerard K. O'Neill and his associates, Box 708, Princeton, New Jersey 08540.

A Timetable

(Real and Imagined)

1957   Russians launch first Earth satellite, Sputnik 1.

1969   Americans Neil Armstrong and Buzz Aldrin become first men to land on moon.

1973   Skylab shows that Earthlings can live in space for prolonged periods.

1974   First large public meeting on space colonization is held at Princeton University.

1977   NASA begins test flights of space shuttle.

1985   After recurrent energy shortages, the President of the United States authorizes solar power satellites to be built in space.

1995   First mining operations on moon begin.

1996   Other countries ask to join the United States in construction of a space colony.

2001   Initial space colony is occupied at L5.

for
Space Colonization

2003 First solar power station built at L5 is placed in Earth orbit and begins beaming microwaves to the ground.

2009 Construction of second-generation space habitats holding as many as 160,000 people begins.

2025 More than ten million people are living at L5.

2035 Space colonies begin tapping raw materials from the asteroid belt.

2046 Two colonies are permanently established in the asteroid belt.

2076 On the tricentennial celebration of United States independence, more Americans are living in space than in their home country on Earth.

2084 Space colonies form a federation of states in space—a virtual declaration of independence from Earth.

2100 Planning begins for sending the first spaceship out of the solar system toward another star.

Index